The Heart & Soul of
Effective Management

The Heart & Soul of
EFFECTIVE MANAGEMENT

JAMES F. HIND

VICTOR BOOKS®

A DIVISION OF SCRIPTURE PRESS PUBLICATIONS INC.
USA CANADA ENGLAND

Recommended Dewey Decimal Classification: 658
Suggested Subject Heading: MANAGEMENT

Library of Congress Catalog Card Number: 89-60147
ISBN: 0-89693-638-4

CONTENTS

Acknowledgements

In the early stages of formulating the concept and developing drafts of this book, I was encouraged and helped greatly by both clergy and businesspeople. The clergy included: the Reverend H. Hunter Huckabay, Jr., D.D., the Reverend Daniel P. Matthews, D.D., the Reverend Charles B. Roberts, and the Right Reverend Bennett J. Sims. The Reverend John Stone Jenkins was most gracious with his time, critique, and prayers. The businesspeople included: James A. Haslam II, Donald R. Mercer, Ralph B. Odman, Patrick O'Donnell, Grantland O'Neal, James Schindler, Michael C. Willard and Dr. Philip G. Wright.

I am indebted to Raymond W. Clark, chairman, Department of Biblical Studies, Covenant College, with whom I spent numerous hours reviewing and discussing the wording used in the text. He taught me much about the meaning of the Gospels, a process which brought me closer to Christ. Dr. J.H.W. Rhys, professor of New Testament, the School of Theology, the University of the South; and Dr. Roger E. Martin, dean, Temple Baptist Theological Seminary gave me a better understanding of Jesus' attitude toward and relationship to the Law.

Susan, my wife, typed and reviewed numerous drafts. Her excitement helped keep the project underway, while her ideas improved the message. Her support and input have been deeply appreciated.

I am especially grateful to Robert N. Hosack for bringing a professional and persuasive touch to the manuscript. The book could not have been written without his editorial expertise and the faith and patience of the management at Victor Books.

All of the forenamed gave unselfishly of their time and knowledge. They truly exemplified the theme of this book, *servant leadership,* helping me to be all that God created me to be.

DEDICATION

To my wife, Susan, a loving companion, a bright business-person, and wise advisor;

To Jim, my son, who is serving others through his own company; and Angela, my daughter, who is serving others through her medical profession;

And in memory of my mother and father.

PART ONE
Introduction

ONE

Bridging the Gap between Church and Boardroom

It is one of those Sundays. The words of the sermon echo over my head. The "stained-glass" saints look my way, but there is no eye contact. The longer the choir sings, "Nearer, My God, to Thee," the more my thoughts wander. My mind is in another world and is racing to itemize a "to be done" list for the coming week. Nothing said, sung, or shown to me that day in church seems relevant to that other world—the world of business.

Driving home, I feel guilty for not being more attentive, for not trying to better understand and relate biblical principles to my world—to make them work in my work. I want to feel what that church hymn is saying.

But the more I ponder my dilemma, the more I realize how wide the gap is between the spiritual world of the church and the secular world of business. What has Christ dying on a cross early in the first century got to do with me trying to achieve economic growth for a company late in the twentieth century?

As a businessman, I have wrestled with that question for thirty years. I find that I am not alone. Most of my peers fail to see a close connection. Few of us are Monday morning disciples. There is an attitude common to professional people that church and business exist in two unrelated worlds—a Sunday one and a workaday one. Christianity is not viewed as an integral part of the business culture.

The chief executive of a large American corporation remarked, "I don't like to go to church on Sunday because it makes me soft and generous—with too much feeling and not enough tough-minded objectivity." This attitude is not too surprising since most companies reward competency, not caring. Qualities of the head—tough-minded realistic thought, are reinforced while qualities of the heart—softness, feeling, and generosity are negated.[1]

Whether monitoring a machine on the factory floor or addressing a board of directors, we are confronted with stresses, strains, and temptations. We often have to compromise and capitulate to succeed in an uncompromising financial world and a survival-of-the-fittest environment. We "go along to get along." There is ample opportunity, but too often little room for sensitivity.

Qualities of the head—tough-minded, realistic thought, that's successful business management. Qualities of the heart—softness, feeling, and generosity, that's successful Christianity. They are worlds apart in a capitalistic society that increasingly rests upon self-interest, economic growth, and their constant expression in the workplace.

There is a big gap between the church altar and the company boardroom. This trend started around the turn of the century when our country's robber barons put power, status, wealth, and themselves above others. The chasm has been widening ever since, as such practices were institutionalized in the American system.

This book attempts to bridge that gap. It is designed to help inspire, inform, equip, and encourage business people in the everyday use of Christian principles in the workplace. It is about returning practical Christianity to the workaday world.

The Approach

Our approach will use Jesus Christ and His teachings as a role model—as a manager to emulate and follow. It begins with a discussion of Christ in the historical context of His mission, message, and meaning. We will study and identify the ways He managed and motivated His disciples. From this we will develop a set of Christian principles for the businessperson to follow—ones that breed productivity in people and make for effective management.

The quest is for a functional and valid approach: one that is true to Christ in an historical context; one that respects the integrity of the Scriptures and Christian experience; and one that appeals to businesspeople as adaptable to the "real" world of commerce.

I have a word of warning before we proceed. To make the approach more meaningful and easier for the professional person to relate to, *I have couched the study of Christ in business language and perspective.* I acknowledge this as a liberty I have taken and hope you'll appreciate and benefit from it.

You may wonder why I chose Jesus of Nazareth, whose earthly walk was almost 2,000 years ago, as a role model for modern management. You may ask how I can reconcile the tremendous cultural differences between then and now. I will answer the "why" question here and the "how" question later.

Why Jesus Christ?

Christ was the most effective executive in the history of the human race. The results He achieved are second to none. In only three years, He defined a mission and formed strategies and plans to carry it out. With a staff of twelve unlikely men, He organized Christianity, which has grown to have 1.5 billion proponents today, is international in scope, and has branches in all the world's 223 countries. Christianity has a 32.4 percent share of the world's current population—twice as big as its nearest rival.[2] He recruited, trained, and motivated twelve ordinary men to become extraordinary. He is the greatest manager and developer of people ever.

We learn by encountering, listening, and responding to other human beings and their life experiences. Jesus Christ was born and reared on our Earth, not on another planet. He grew in wisdom and in stature as He lived as one of us. His human experience was broad and varied.

In His lifetime, He worked and associated with all types of people ranging from the unsophisticated, peasant poor, and ridiculed outcasts to the highly educated, respected and influential, and powerfully rich.

He had to contend with the agendas of various political, civil, and religious authorities—some with the highest integrity, but many with the lowest duplicity. These experiences gave Jesus a keen perception of and profound insight into human nature. Nothing about people's attitudes or actions was too small or common to escape His attention.

His parables show He was a man of many interests. The wisdom they impart show that Jesus had a remarkable intellect and extraordinary skills as a teacher.

Executives study the management qualities of history's great business leaders. It seems as if every other month is marked by a high profile CEO's new book promising to pave the way to business success. Business people sometimes seem captivated by the latest fad or newest trend.

Doesn't it make equal sense to examine the experiences and teachings of a successful person such as Jesus Christ? To study His corporate culture (beliefs and behavior), management style, and understanding of human nature is to begin an unparalleled adventure in learning.

Those individuals and companies that can learn to build

their management beliefs and behavior around Christian principles bring a sense of special significance to the workplace, a high quality of integrity that gives people a stronger ethic and motivation to do their work well.

Lawrence Miller, a long-time business consultant to "blue-chip" companies, describes it this way in *American Spirit: Visions of a New Corporate Culture.* He is answering the questions: why do some managers possess the quality of integrity while others do not—and where and by whom is this integrity created?

> It is my experience and the experience of other observers that managers who inspire devotion have dedication to a higher, sometimes mysterious, perhaps spiritual purpose. They believe in a course, a reason, and a set of truths beyond their control and to which everything else must conform. These beliefs may be in God or religion, but it is always in a superior force or truth. It is the adherence to these beliefs and the mission to carry them forward that provides an internal security that allows them to behave with integrity. Their beliefs provide them with a sense of special significance which is the key to their leadership. They know that they are not merely serving themselves, a goal for which they know little is worth sacrificing, but they are serving their cause, mission, or faith, for which great sacrifices are justified. Employees have an unspoken sensitivity to this spiritual significance and respond in a way that results in meaning within their own lives.[3]

O.A. Ohmann, psychology professor and managerial developer, has written of similar trends. Many great executives have a deep internal resource from which they draw strength in tough times. Ohmann refers to this as a "skyhook." It is a devotion to a higher purpose or calling. The "skyhook" provides a sense of connection which brings calm and confidence in the hectic business climate.[4]

This book proposes that "skyhook" be a spiritual purpose: the everyday use of Christian principles in managing and motivating people in the workplace.

Swing on This Skyhook!

For the Christian businessperson, this "skyhook" provides a way of taking biblical principles learned in Sunday's church hour into the weekday hours of the workaday world. Values learned in the church must be in harmony with those practiced on the job, if we are to be whole and healthy personalities. When our values are in conflict, disillusionment and dissatisfaction set in.

For those who are looking to become better managers (or more effective mentors), the "skyhook" will help. It shows how to integrate softness, feeling, and generosity with tough-minded, realistic thought, and motivate people for significantly increased productivity. For those who are looking for greater satisfaction on the job (and I suspect that is most of us), this "skyhook" provides that—and that is its greatest benefit.

As a senior executive, it will answer your questions: "Is this all there is? Is there not something more rewarding?" If you are in middle management and clawing your way up the ladder of success, it will show you different and more gratifying ways of achieving that success. If you have just graduated or are newly starting in the world of business, using these Christian principles of management will accelerate your development. And if you have grown cold and stale in the same old job every day, hanging on to this "skyhook" will renew you.

Accept the challenge! Hook on to this piece of sky. Swing on this "skyhook." Learn how to happily succeed at your job with rewards far greater than your expectations—ones that are everlasting.

Two
Giving Soul to American Business

"We have tried man's way. It has failed. Now it is time to try God's way." That was the viewpoint of Wayne Alderson, a newly appointed vice president in charge of operations at Pittron Steel, a steel foundry in Glassport, Pennsylvania.[1]

The year was early 1973, and Alderson was faced with a previous three year loss of $6 million and an on-going strike that threatened to shut down the company permanently. He settled the strike, and now he had to keep the promises he made to labor with visible and genuine action. He had "talked the talk"; now it was time to "walk the walk."

That was not an easy task. The hostility of the steel workers had long been evolving and was deeply embedded. The hearts of the workers had been hardened by years of deplorable working conditions, their loss of dignity under an aloof and hostile management, and a string of broken promises.

The union was tough, argued the old management, and we have to be tougher.

Alderson challenged these traditional management techniques, feeling that to return to the old system would be to return to what was no longer valid or effective. He knew, though, he had to retain the best of the old (competency, discipline, excellence, and hard work) while implementing some innovative measures.

He conceived a bold and innovative plan to earn the workers' trust, to improve their morale, and to make the company productive and profitable. He called it Operation Turnaround. It was founded on the idea that while companies should not operate as churches, their management through their decisions and actions were still fully accountable to God.

At the forefront of his plan was reconciliation with the workers, and Alderson showed the way to his management team. He stood at the company gate, and as the men came off the shift, thanked each for their day's work—something never done before at Pittron. He walked the factory floor, addressed the men by name and chatted with them about their work problems—a far cry from the style of the previous management that insisted such discussion and dialogue take place only over a negotiating table. He gave the union president, the leader on the floor, an office in which to meet with his men. He eliminated the negative criticism of workers by management, that "red pencil" mentality which produces fear and resentment, rather than respect. He encouraged and motivated the factory workers with genuine and deserving compliments.

With these small but meaningful gestures, Operation Turnaround began to come about and at its core emerged Alderson's "Value of the Person" concept. Alderson realized that he had found something all men and women at Pittron had in common: they all wanted to be valued. He then identified the three key ingredients that were necessary to make this "Value of the Person" concept succeed. They were love, dignity, and respect. He understood that worker morale and reconciliation come from the way people are treated. He had so often heard the many slogans centered around the idea of, "We put people first," but so many times saw them become forgotten words, lying dead on a wall poster as soon as production or profit pressures became great. Through the giving of love, dignity, and respect to his workers, he realized he could give full meaning to his "Value of the Person" concept.

In the months that followed, the management team emphasized and practiced these underlying principles through daily, concrete actions with their workers and each other. Alderson visited their homes in time of trouble. He was at the hospital when someone was hurt, at the funeral parlor when someone died. When the "energy crunch" hit the nation in 1974 and there were long lines and high prices at the gas pumps, he provided his workers with free gas based on the honor system—no questions asked.

There was a new spirit moving among the workers and it was more than just teamwork and camaraderie between labor and management. In the most antiquated, grimy room of the foundry, the workers at their own request began to meet together and hold an informal Bible study during their lunch hour. Wayne Alderson led the discussion.

But don't be mistaken about Wayne Alderson. He was not a clergyman in the foundry. Operation Turnaround was not intended to be a religious program. Attendance at the chapel under-the-open-hearth was strictly voluntary. Nevertheless, God's ways were working through Wayne Alderson, a man with deep Christian vision and faith.

What did all this accomplish? Pittron became more than a nice place to work; measurable results were recorded. In only twenty-one months, Wayne Alderson and his "Value of the Person" program moved Pittron from a deficit of $6 million to a profit of $6 million, a profit-loss swing of $12 million.

Alderson's story is living proof that God's ways can succeed in the workplace, even in the worst of business situations. His "Value of the Person" program strikes at the very heart of the approach proposed in this book: *the belief that all people have inherent value by virtue of being created in the image of God, and thus an inherent right to develop to their fullest potential.*[2] Such a perspective promotes a "caring" attitude that commits you to using work to help people develop and succeed—rather than using people to accomplish work so that you and your company may succeed.

A Few Have It

Some American companies have a caring management approach, more are striving for it, but most don't have it. Where it is strongly promoted it usually reflects the philosophy of the founder, chairman, or chief executive officer.

Sam Walton, Chairman of the Board and Chief Executive Officer of Wal-Mart, a discount retailer with over 200,000 employees, is a good example. When Walton started Wal-Mart, he felt that creating an atmosphere of partnership in the business would work a lot better than the traditional employer-employee relationship. So he and his management refer to their people as "associates," emphasizing people development, participatory management, and open communications. "Our People Make the Difference" is the company's slogan. Sam, tabbed America's richest, often drives a pickup truck to meet his company's prominent visitors.

In their 1988 Annual Report, their Chief Operating Officer, Don Soderquist, espoused this philosophy:

> Every associate is an individual with certain God-given talents and abilities. If they are treated with respect and dignity and they are allowed to use their talents and abilities, we can accomplish far more together than any of us could if left alone to develop and operate our own store. Although we fail many times, it's so important that we work together, that we treat each other like we would

like to be treated, that we really care about each other.[3]

Wal-Mart is highly successful not only in the caring and development of people but also in maximizing growth and profits. Wal-Mart is one of the fastest growing major retailers in the country with an annual rate of growth compounded over the past ten years at close to 40 percent in sales and 40 percent in profits.[4]

Another strong example is the late Marion Wade, the founder of The ServiceMaster Company, a management services firm that runs its billion dollar business on Christian principles. Wade had a unique philosophy for his business people: "We must become servants, first of all of the Lord, and then, in His name, servants unto all. We must serve."[5] The company is committed to being masters of service, serving the Master, and thus the firm's name—ServiceMaster.

Starting as a rug and furniture cleaning service for homes and offices in the 1950s, ServiceMaster has expanded into supportive management services for health care, educational, and industrial facilities. Recently it has become a leader in providing professional cleaning and pest control services to homes and businesses. The company operates in major countries throughout the world.

It is a thriving example of a corporation with a caring management approach. To my knowledge it is the only large public firm that explicitly states such a perspective. It is evidenced in their first two corporate objectives: "to honor God in all we do . . . [and] to help people develop."[6] In today's business arena, ServiceMaster is a remarkable company with a remarkable philosophy—and it is working.

Author's Note: The Wal-Mart and ServiceMaster examples are not meant to imply that a company or individual with religious devotion is guaranteed economic prosperity. The rewards of Christianity are not economic success. They go far beyond that and are more satisfying. What Wal-Mart and ServiceMaster do show is that capitalism and Christian principles can be intimately related and work together successfully—even in the larger firms of business America.

While it places growing profitably as its *last* corporate objective (after God, people, and the pursuit of excellence), it has placed *first* in profits on a list of 500 nonindustrial companies. *Fortune* magazine reports, "The most profitable company in the last ten years—indeed the jewel among all 1,000 companies in the service and industrial lists combined—was ServiceMaster."[7]

The company's phenomenal growth has been reflected in the performance of its stock splitting seven times and its dividend increasing thirty-two times in the last fifteen years. Success continued in 1988—ServiceMaster had record revenue and earnings.[8]

ServiceMaster believes its success comes largely from their leader-managers' care and concern for people development and the company's commitment to remaining unified through the stresses and joys of achieving its goals.[9]

Most Don't Have It

For every American company that practices such a caring attitude, there are thousands that don't. And the management styles and behavior of their executives clearly demonstrate it.

Fortune magazine annually publishes a story on "The Toughest Bosses in America." Candidates are based on multiple nominations from a broad representation of the business community. *Fortune* then interviews people who currently or in the past have worked for the candidates, especially those who have firsthand knowledge of how candidates treat their subordinates. Only when a consensus emerges does a candidate become a finalist. Following are some enlightening descriptions of these superiors, the executive management of some of America's top companies.[10]

● Senior Executive, Conglomerate: All stick and not much carrot . . . Has all the answers and thinks everybody is a _____head . . . His attitude is, why change when I'm being rewarded for everything I do.

- Chairman, Large Conglomerate: High IQ, very abrasive, doesn't want "I think" answers ... I've never met a man with so many creative business ideas. I've never felt that anybody was tapping my brain so well ... He's a high-strung instrument. Misses the opportunity to get input from people who don't have the skill or courage to play him like a violin ... Too determined to get a notch on his six-gun ... Working for him is like a war. A lot of people get shot up; the survivors go on to the next battle.

- Chairman, Large Manufacturer of Machinery and Chemicals: Bright, gets quickly to the nub of an issue, but can be punitive ... Below top management ranks he's perceived as a bully ... Intensely persistent.

- Chairman, Large Oil Company: Comes across as having a Napoleon complex—he has to throw his weight around ... Imperious ... Unwilling to entertain ideas that don't fit in with his.

- Chairman, Large Textile Company: Unable to communicate or praise people ... The smartest guy I've ever met in the textile industry, but cold and, some would say, ruthless ... Not much room for original thought at his company ... He has seldom admitted a mistake, and he has never hesitated to make subordinates pay for them.

- Chairman, Utility Company: Incredible egomaniac ... Cold ... Those who have stayed with him are the kind who can get used to working with a self-proclaimed genius ... In dealing with _____, you can't have an ego of your own ... Unbelievably litigious ... Fair ... He has underpaid everybody equally.

- Chief Executive, Large Conglomerate: Probably one of the most demanding people in the world. Yells, curses when he chews people out ... Employees scared to death of him.

● Chief Executive, Large Conglomerate: Favorite retort when anyone questions a decision, "If you're so smart, why aren't you rich?" Wild temper tantrums and firing threats commonplace.

The preceding comments are eye-opening. Where is the "Value of the Person" concept that respects inherent human value? Where is love, dignity, and respect for others? They are not evident in the preceding management styles. Even *Fortune* disagrees with such management styles: "In an era of Theory Z and one minute praisings, this kind of behavior is out of fashion. What does it accomplish? Making a case for it on economic grounds is hard when financial results from these bosses' companies vary from superb to pathetic."[1]

This broad sample of management, my thirty years of business experience, and data and examples from Main Street to Wall Street all point to the same conclusion: the self-centered, "uncaring" attitude toward managing people is common and spreading. It seems as if Sam Walton and Marion Wade are the uncommon ones.

From the basement to the boardroom, there is little attention paid to managing and motivating the human nature of people. Their natural instincts, appetites, and ambitions are neglected. Such an environment fails to create the changes in mind, heart, and attitude necessary for people, along with the company, to succeed to the fullest.

Too often, managers, verbally as well as nonverbally, communicate an uncaring attitude to their people. "I know you—but I don't have time for you" is a common impression. Many managers act like the pin-striped executive who responds to his subordinates, "Yes, I do know the name of the serviceman in the Tomb of the Unknown Soldier. Any further disagreement should be put in writing, in the same envelope as your resignation."

And in graduate business schools across America, most curriculums omit practical courses on managing people to help them develop personally *and* succeed professionally.

One critic notes, "Too many MBA's are taught to treat ordinary employees as disposable 'direct labor cost.' They are taught to swallow uncritically the myth that corporations exist only to reward abstract stockholders, that capital budgeting and financial controls are the most effective management tools."[12]

Business books, videos, and seminars emphasize achieving excellence, creating innovation, managing change, learning to lead, power strategies, negotiating, and finance. Most focus on self-development, to benefit one's own interest and welfare. Few, if any, focus on helping the other person develop and succeed. A recent national poll shows these same priorities in the minds of the majority of college students going into the business world![13]

Business America has neglected our Lord's second greatest commandment: "Love your neighbor as yourself."[14]

Why Is This Happening?
There are a number of reasons for American business' disregard. First and foremost, we have strayed from honoring God in our business life. In disobeying His commands, we develop a secular purpose focusing only on ourselves.

Social theorist Robert Nisbet talks about this progression of self-interest in our business society:

> What was so easily called "self-interest" was in the beginning and indeed in the subsequent history of this economic system until a short while ago much more than that. It was self-interest, if we like, but it was inseparable from the restraints which sprang from a religious and moral atmosphere that was at one time highly influential. "Economic man" was in fact being strongly driven by or held back by considerations which were not economic at all and which were once strongly influential. These moral and spiritual values have, however, become weakened.[15]

Robert Bachelder sees the same root problem and refers to this decline of moral and spiritual values as "the lost soul of American business."[16]

This moral malaise is being accelerated by a host of new issues which make business more competitive and complex than ever before. I believe there are five crucial factors influencing these changes:

1. An age of high tech that puts machine efficiency ahead of people.
2. Government deregulation by which companies are meeting a different type of competition and having to redefine their mission and methodology.
3. Hostile and friendly takeovers where employees and stockholders usually lose and management, with their always "golden parachutes" (guaranteed take-away pay), and insiders on Wall Street are the only winners.
4. Growth of conglomerates where new corporate cultures become mixed with old—often confusing and intimidating to employees.
5. Global competition where imports with lower prices, equal or better quality, are forcing American companies to be more efficient or go out of business.

These factors, and the pressures they create, are causing management to shift away from a caring attitude for people and to concentrate solely on economic growth and survival of the fittest. Without this caring attitude, there is no longer a covenant of good faith and fair dealing between the employee and the boss or the employee and the company's policies. There is no credible atmosphere for trust to succeed.

This breakdown has led to a disruption of the workplace and lives of people. Employee turnover runs high as people question their career future and happiness in what becomes an intimidating and less than productive work environment. The result is a corporate loyalty crisis. Corporate America's best and brightest are leaving to start their own businesses. The average American professional is changing jobs every three years and the maintenance of dual careers is becoming common. Skilled and semiskilled workers are being forced to abandon their trades, to take lower paying, less demanding jobs, as the nation shifts from an industrial to a service economy. This upheaval has caused people to ask more questions about the meaning of their work.[17]

Interviewee Nora Watson clearly expressed it to Studs Terkel in his book *Working:* "I think most of us are looking for a calling, not a job. Most of us, like the assembly line worker, have jobs that are too small for our spirit. Jobs are not big enough for people."[18]

What Is Needed?

Business America needs a "calling," a fresh and meaningful approach to managing the human nature of people. It must be one that appreciates and promotes people's self-worth and their value to each other. And it must use work to help people develop and succeed if it is to vie profitably in an increasingly competitive business environment. Otherwise, business will be reduced to a lost soul, insensitive to people's needs, marked by power structures and bank accounts, and driven by self-interest and economic considerations alone.

This book proposes a new and different approach for people to manage themselves and others. It proposes a meaningful and motivating framework that makes it work. I'm suggesting a revolutionary type of leadership for the American manager—one that returns spiritual values to the workplace and gives people a "calling."

Robert H. Waterman, Jr., coauthor of the best-selling management book of all time, *In Search of Excellence*, has written a new book, *The Renewal Factor: How the Best Get*

THE HEART AND SOUL OF EFFECTIVE MANAGEMENT

and Keep the Competitive Edge. He stresses the importance of management making the work challenging to people and helping them to believe in their individual worth. He illustrates it with a story: Three people were at work on a construction site. All were doing the same job, but when each was asked what his job was, the answers varied. "Breaking rocks," the first replied. "Earning my living," said the second. "Helping to build a cathedral," said the third.[19]

Most of us want to feel that we are building cathedrals in our work, not just muddling through until payday. The pages that follow will suggest an approach to help us find those cathedrals.

PART TWO

The Approach

THREE

Jesus Christ:
The Role Model

The Apostle Paul's story is a classic example of what can happen to a man under new management. As Saul, before he met Christ, he was a legalistic interpreter of the Law and merciless persecutor of the Christian way. After his spectacular conversion, he had not only a new name, Paul, but new management as well.

He was transformed from a selfish defender of his old religious ways to a tireless promoter of the new Christian religion. As a leader in the early church, he encouraged followers of the Way to be like-minded, one in spirit and purpose: "Do nothing out of selfish ambition or vain conceit, but in humility consider others better than yourselves. Each of you should look not only to your own interests, but also to the interests of others."[1]

Paul promoted people working together and serving one

another—teamwork as we know it in our workaday world. He was not saying consider others to be superior in intellect or talent, but to see others as worthy of preferential treatment. The basis for this is Christian love as we know it in our church world. Paul means that our own interests are proper, but only if there is equal concern for the interests of others. With such a Golden Rule approach, there is no room for selfish ambition and vain conceit.

Paul expressed his convictions in a well-known passage describing Jesus:

> Your attitude should be the same as that of Christ Jesus: Who, being in very nature God, did not consider equality with God something to be grasped, but made Himself nothing, taking the very nature of a servant, being made in human likeness. And being found in appearance as a man, He humbled Himself and became obedient to death—even death on a cross! Therefore God exalted Him to the highest place and gave Him the name that is above every name, that at the name of Jesus every knee should bow, in heaven and on earth and under the earth, and every tongue confess that Jesus Christ is Lord, to the glory of the Father.[2]

Christ the Servant, Christ the Man

Christ who is the very essence of God Himself laid aside His glory and deity and took on the nature of a servant. He adopted the appearance and likeness of a man.

As a servant He met the needs of others, always obedient to the will of His Father, even to the point of death on a cross. As a human being, He humbled Himself before others, and was crucified as a common criminal in the most agonizing form of death ever invented by man.

It is this servant process which Christ so faithfully followed in His attitude, teachings, and actions toward the people and issues of His day that will be our role model. We will focus on the *human side* of Christ, developing a Christian approach to managing and motivating people.

I believe strongly in the two distinct natures of Christ—His deity and humanity. First and foremost, "Christ was deity in the highest sense, possessed of all attributes and titles of God and free of any taint of sin or error."[3] I believe as it says in that great historic creed of the church that Jesus was "very God of very God, begotten, not made, being of one substance with the Father."[4]

But as I have studied and reflected on the Scriptures, conversed with lay people and clergy alike, and experienced the ups and downs of life, I have also come to appreciate and identify with the humanity of Christ. As I read about the physical side of His human nature—His birth, growth, fatigue, suffering, and death—I realize that "Christ was [indeed] bone of our bone and flesh of our flesh."[5]

I can relate to the emotional and devotional sides of Christ. He was open to temptation, but was devoted to prayer. He could be full of joy, yet at times be deep in sorrow. He had the warmest compassion for people, but could get very angry with their actions. He could show love and more love, yet there is no record of Him showing hate. All these sides of Christ help me to see and appreciate the humanity of Christ.

I feel close to Christ when I remember He is someone I can comfortably relate to and confide in as a friend. I rediscover this when I read of Him interacting with people and situations in ways I do so daily. In those moments I learn the most about Him. It's also when I can learn the most from Him.

I believe this can be true for most of us. Thus, I have chosen to emphasize the reactions and experiences of Jesus Christ in dealing with the people and issues of His day—those which are common to our human nature. Even though Christ lived 2,000 years ago in a culture quite different from ours, He was indeed speaking of things applicable to men and women of all times. His principles are timeless, because human nature was the same then as it is now.

His Mission and Message

At the early age of twelve, Jesus' teaching in the temple demonstrated that He was following an inner call from God. This was the first sign that Jesus had a definite mission. His mission was to be about His Father's business. Jesus had work to do; He was to proclaim the coming of the kingdom.

All successful companies have a mission; most offer a unique selling proposition (USP). By purchasing their product or service, the consumer will benefit greatly. Without doing His kingdom mission injustice, we might say that Jesus had a sort of USP. He invited people to repent, follow Him, and experience a kingdom lifestyle that offered a more rewarding way to think, work, and feel about everyday life.

The kingdom of God was a new thing on earth, but Jesus didn't believe that human beings should simply wait for the glorious course of events to come about. He insisted that it could only grow if men and women developed an attitude receptive to God's kingdom. He taught that a complete change of mind and heart (repentance) was needed—a turning away from self to God. This was the message of Christ, and He set out to call people to faith through His life and actions.

Jesus' way was paved by the Prophet John the Baptist, one of His peers. In some ways the two men were alike, in many ways different. Both proclaimed the coming of the kingdom of God. But they were vastly different in their attitudes toward managing and motivating human nature.

John the Baptist lived and spoke a life of protest. He preached boldly, forcefully advancing the kingdom of God. He claimed all mankind was "bound" to repent in light of God's coming kingdom. His words were simple, straight to the point, and tough-minded. His judgment was harsh. He never adjusted his approach or softened his words to make them more appealing to the needs of people.[6]

Jesus Christ lived and spoke a life of reconciliation. Jesus challenged but seldom pushed His listeners. His teachings were often delivered in colorful parables with a wealth of illustrations. He varied His approach according to the character and needs of His audience. He had a knack for sympathizing with human weakness and dealt gently with those who went astray.

Given these striking differences, along with the very strong rivalry of being close in age, one would hardly think these two men could have cooperated with each other. However, they did. John, putting his own importance aside, acknowledged the leadership and primacy of Jesus—without a trace of jealousy. Jesus, humble in heart, affirmed John the Baptist and publicly recognized the accomplishments of His peer. It was brotherhood and teamwork at its best, and it prepared the way for the mission of Jesus Christ.

Jesus, though, like most leaders with a bold new message of change, was challenged and tested early on in His mission. In business parlance, His key competitor was Satan, who tried to lure Him away from His Father's business with more lucrative offers. One was for a higher position that would make Him lord of all the world's kingdoms (the world's largest conglomerate!)—the most prized place of leadership. Satan tried to sell Jesus on accepting this offer by pointing out the power and glory that went with managing the world's kingdoms. It was a cosmic struggle on the highest level, a "power play" forced upon Jesus by Satan. Would Jesus continue to be about His Father's business or yield to temptation and serve Satan?

For our purposes here, that is, focusing on the humanity of Christ, we need to note the personal choice Jesus had to make in His earthly life: Would He continue as a servant, meeting people's needs, or would He yield to promoting personal ambitions and forget the concerns of others? Jesus saw this "fine print" requirement in Satan's contract and promptly turned the offer down. Promoting His own interests for control, ahead of the needs of others, was not part of the mission and message of Jesus Christ.

His Meaning and Market

In the Master's plan for spreading His Father's kingdom, Jesus realized He would have to strategically locate and delegate if the Good News was to reach the masses. He set up His headquarters in Capernaum on the shore of the Sea of Galilee in Palestine within close reach to over 100,000 people. The Capernaum area was the Southern California of its day, acting as a popular magnet for new movements. Jesus chose to begin there before going on to Jerusalem. National religious policy was set and controlled in Jerusalem, the established marketplace for religion, where the real test of His "profession" would come.

Some of the most educated and influential men of opinion lived in Jerusalem. They belonged to proud religious parties. One, the Pharisees, though small in numbers, enjoyed great prestige and were the recognized leaders of the people. They emphasized the rigid rules of religion—policies and procedures to perform along with the do's and don'ts of success.[7]

Another group, the scribes, assisted the Pharisees. They were not priests but laymen who interpreted and taught these rigid rules called the Law. The Law covered ethical, legal, and ritualistic matters; the scribes were the ultimate authority in all matters of faith and practice. The scribes expected the common people to pay them every honor.[8]

According to the Pharisees, God had given Israel the oral and the written Law (the Ten Commandments), that is, the Law with all its interpretations and applications. The prevailing system, however, went much further and allowed the scribes to develop their own class of rules. These were to prevent any violation of the Law, ensure that it was precisely followed, and meet unusual circumstances and temptations.[9]

To many, these rules were hard to understand and even harder to apply in everyday life. To make matters worse, the Pharisees and scribes criticized the masses who failed to uphold the Law as unloyal to God. This was a put-down of the common people, and Jesus did not accept it.

The Pharisees and scribes directed their followers along the lines of authority and obedience, even to the smallest details. People were expected to follow all their legalistic dictates according to the letter of the Law. These religious parties can be compared to management which is "calling all the shots." No effort was made to get feedback from people as to their real feelings and needs. In modern language, there was no participative management. Clearly, the scribes and Pharisees were the corporate structure of religion—imposing difficult rules, driven by self-importance, insensitive to the real issues and needs of people—and Jesus said so loud and clear.

While Jesus had sharp disagreement with the sayings of the scribes and the practices of the Pharisees, He respected the Law. He did not want to abolish it. He wanted to fulfill it—and He did so. Jesus taught that the Good News of the kingdom of God is obedience to the Lord not through a set of rules, but through a relationship to a person, Himself, the Son of God, who has a human (as well as divine) understanding, and relates compassionately to the real concerns of people.

Jesus brought "softness, feeling, and generosity" to the "tough-minded, realistic thoughts" of the Law to inspire and enlist people's devotions. Jesus believed the Law had less to do with external observances than it did with internal attitudes. He felt that if it is written on one's heart—that is, tied to feelings of concern and caring—then it becomes a matter of personal disposition, and naturally inspires an obedient devotion.

Midst this religious milieu, another party, smaller than the Pharisees but still very powerful because of its status and wealth, were the Sadducees. They held most all of the higher religious offices. They directed worship in the temple and controlled the sales organization outside it, charging exorbitant prices for their goods and services. Jesus saw them as they were, men who promoted their own self-interests and worshiped money and profits rather than God.

Religious groups such as the Pharisees, scribes, and Sadducees comprised only about 7 percent of an estimated 800,000 people in Palestine where Christ's mission started.[10] Outside Palestine in the Mediterranean area lived millions of people of diverse nationalities and religions. Some worshiped Olympian gods, household deities, or local pagan folk heroes. Others worshiped the supernatural through sorcerers, seances, and omens. Many, though, were disillusioned with and strongly indifferent to religion.[11]

I find the fact that Jesus Christ could create an appeal for Christianity in such an apathetic environment to be the most remarkable example in history of understanding human nature and motivating people to willing action. To understand how He did it and discover what we can learn from His example is our challenge. Granted, ushering in the kingdom of God cannot compare with running a business, but the timeless principles of human understanding we can gain from studying Jesus will be forever applicable to managing people everywhere.

FOUR
Jesus Christ:
The Manager

According to John MacArthur, there was no "executive search" when Christ selected His management team—the disciples.¹ Jesus chose very ordinary men in terms of their intellect and economic and social backgrounds. They were humble villagers, simple and sincere, naive to an outside world ruled by the rich, powerful, crafty, and wise.

They did though, like all people, have feelings and wills of their own. And Christ knew that ordinary people have extraordinary potential. The disciples weren't "know it all" types. They were teachable—sometimes slow to learn and quick to overreact—but nonetheless teachable.

First, as His students, they learned as He coached and counseled them. Then, as His assistants and associates, they participated in practical work assignments. Finally, as His management team, they traveled far and wide in influencing and persuading people to accept God's kingdom.

Jesus' manner and method of training differed from the orthodox teachers of His time. They quoted authority. He spoke with authority. They taught strictly from a book. He gave new insights to the book and disagreed with the accepted understanding of it. He taught by example—marching His disciples through the hills and valleys of Palestine, with actions that made His teachings come alive. He was the Master teacher and they were His select students. He nurtured them as disciples so they in turn could help others develop.

While the teachers kept their distances from the common people, Jesus aggressively went among them. He especially enjoyed intimate fellowship with His disciples. He talked, walked, and prayed with them on the back roads and in crowded cities and on the Sea of Galilee.

Further, the traditional teachers stressed intellect. Jesus, on the other hand, stressed compassion—that deep feeling of sharing in the suffering of another. Jesus judged people first with His heart, not His head. He showed His disciples how much He cared before He showed them how much He knew, because Jesus Christ felt that affairs of the heart rather than of the mind were the key issues in people's lives.

He paid close and caring attention to the individual weaknesses of the disciples and tailored His advice and counsel accordingly, always addressing the issue and never "dressing down" the person. He interested them in what they could be, promoting and changing their expectations of success. In doing so, He changed their behavior, and they achieved far beyond their abilities.

What follows are some major examples of how Christ did this. Over a three-year period of continuous and concentrated training, He made ordinary men extraordinary.

Peter
Peter was a "mover and shaker," always initiating and trying to make things happen. He had a strong sense of urgency

to get things done. His motto could have easily been: If you don't make dust, you'll eat dust.

Impulsive and inquisitive, Peter asked Jesus more questions than all the others combined. But Peter was a thoughtful questioner seeking answers that could help him better understand and grow—and better "sell" the ways of Jesus. Christ recognized this and He gave Peter thoughtful replies.

Peter often asked a tough "make or break the business" question: If we leave everything and follow You, what then shall we have? He wanted to know the bottom line upfront.

Christ replied that His way was not always the easiest, but it was the most rewarding. He went on to say that no one ever gave up anything for Him who did not get it back a hundredfold. But He added some words of caution on who would be rewarded: "But many who are first will be last, and the last first."[2]

Peter, the bold leader of the group, was probably assessing his own worth and reward too highly. Jesus pointed out to him that a person may stand high in the judgment of the world, but find that God's evaluation is very different.[3]

It was not a warning against achieving personal success. It pointed out the pitfalls of having an excessively high opinion of one's self in achieving that success. Such an attitude often leads to conceit and arrogance and lording it over others. Neither was it a warning against obtaining possessions and wealth. It was a clear statement of fact that God's measurements of greatness are not the world's standards.

No doubt about it, Jesus saw the leadership strengths in Peter: his ability to ask the right questions, his decisiveness, his courage, and his strong belief in the mission of the Lord. But Jesus did not overlook the many weaknesses in Peter.

Peter was not always dependable. Jesus, knowing the Pharisees were looking for Him, asked Peter to watch while He prayed. Peter went to sleep along with the others. Christ singled Peter out. Jesus was questioning Peter's spirit of service and suggested that he pray for a more hearty one.

Peter lost his self-control at times. When Jesus peacefully

told the Pharisees' arresting party that He was the One for whom they were looking, Peter hastily drew his sword and cut off the right ear of the high priest's servant. Jesus politely told Peter that God was in control, and He didn't need his assistance at that time.

Peter was unpredictable and difficult to manage at times. He told Jesus he would never have his feet washed by Him (a lesson of humble service), then he turned right around and asked Jesus to wash his entire body. Three times Jesus patiently explained to Peter and the others this act of selfless service to others.

Peter told Jesus he would lay down his life for Him; then almost in the next breath disowned Him. It was this human weakness, this incident of "fleeting faith," where Christ could have washed His hands of Peter, but He didn't. It became the turning point in Peter's life.

After three years of profitable ministry, Peter saw Jesus facing a sudden and complete collapse of power. Peter still believed in what Christ was teaching, but he was not willing to risk his reputation by acknowledging Him in front of others. Peter lacked the courage of his convictions. He began to play the "avoid and aloof" game—keeping his distance from Christ. In much the same way business people often treat others who are losing their "power position" or job. When Peter's real test came, he would not even acknowledge, much less support, his "boss." He chose the safe way to avoid being arrested as a supporter of Christ's teachings.

Peter went from a backslapper to a backslider. He lost the following of his peers and eventually his position in the disciples' company. He was forced to return to his previous occupation. But Jesus did not say, "I told you so." His concern and care for people was such that He wanted to help them, even when their problems were a result of their own weaknesses. He didn't kick a man when he was down. He accompanied His challenge—"Follow Me!"—with support for those who dared to try.

Jesus supported Peter in his most critical crisis. After Christ's resurrection, He overlooked Peter's denial and reinstated him in His service. Under Jesus' tutelage, Peter slowly and painfully developed those qualities which He sought to instill in him. Peter became not only the spokesman for the Twelve, but also their leader. Known as the "rock," he was to become a future source of strength in expanding God's kingdom business.

James and John

James and John were brothers selected by Christ. They turned out to be overly ambitious managers who in a power play tried to organize the disciples' power structure so that James would sit at Christ's right and John at Christ's left in heaven. In today's terms, it was "office politics" at its worst.

Being deceptively outwitted, it was natural for the rest of the group to be mad and jealous. And like anyone involved in a rumored reorganization, they became tense and anxious to know what was going to happen to them. So Jesus called them all together. Instead of announcing a reorganization of management, He encouraged a reorganization of their mindset. He scorned the idea of power and authority over others as a virtue. He emphasized that the only real greatness is—not to be served—but to serve others.

He went on to say the leadership positions, the promotions James and John wanted, were not His to grant. They can't be assigned on the basis of favoritism. They have to be won through performance—through service to others.

John continued to need help developing as a manager. His selfish ambition sometimes made him narrow in his tolerance of others. He once criticized a man who did not mirror his image—who did not dress, think, nor manage like him—yet was getting the job done. " 'Teacher,' said John, 'we saw a man driving out demons in Your name and we told him to stop, because he was not one of us.' "[4]

John seems to have jealously labeled the man a lightweight, weak in style and approach, because he was not a member of the "glorious company" of twelve. Christ differed with John and quickly set him straight, warning against putting labels on others and disregarding their attitude and performance. John eventually changed his perspective, grew in his consideration for others, and passionately became devoted to Jesus.

Andrew

Peter's brother, Andrew, had been a follower of John the Baptist. With John the Baptist's endorsement, Andrew joined the company of Christ and became one of the Twelve.

Unlike Peter, Andrew had no driving ambitions to fame. He was not a leader but more of a "contact" man, an intermediary, a very approachable and pleasant person with whom to work. More than once he saw that the right people got to see Jesus at the right time. He introduced Peter to Jesus. He brought the boy with the loaves and fishes to Jesus to feed the hungry. Andrew even helped outsiders who were "serious seekers," but shunned by many, to get an interview with Jesus. He was always looking out for others.

Andrew was not a high-profile executive. He was a middle management type who labored quietly but got the job done. Christ recognized Andrew's concern for others and his low-key way of managing and often included him in important meetings and events.

He was simple in character and sought no prominence, but Andrew is still held in honor throughout the Christian world. He was one of those who seemed to be last but was really first.

Matthew

Matthew was a "numbers" man, concerned with the bottom line and not particularly people-oriented. He administered the corrupt and wasteful system of collecting taxes. This job was sold to the highest bidder, and thus Matthew made his profit by charging as much above his cost as the traffic would bear. He had a good financial mind, but a bad reputation because of his lowly occupation and the rumored way he treated people. Society scorned him and refused to socialize with him. Few cared for him or his occupation as tax collector.

Despite this, Christ pardoned Matthew's "money-worshiping" and visited his house for dinner. Christ, as a manager, had no walls of aloofness around Him, even for the "lower" levels. He went out of His way to socialize and to actively and publically recognize the needs of others. Christ was in the business of changing lives. He helped people succeed beyond their own desires and expectations. Matthew was a prime candidate for the personal touch Jesus offered.

As Matthew spent more time with Jesus, he became even richer, not in money, but in ideas and deeds—going from a collector of taxes to a distributor of these riches. Church tradition believes Matthew was the first to give the world a book on Jesus' teachings. It brought him God's measurement of greatness, servanthood—far beyond the wealth of money and possessions.

Thomas

Then there was "doubting Thomas," who failed to grasp the meaning of Christ's teachings and actions and doubted without seeing actual proof. Thomas did not have a lot of vision. His understanding of how Jesus could establish and expand God's kingdom was limited.

He was an "I'll believe it when I see it" manager. In the group's meetings, he was often the pessimist, questioning the possibility of a favorable outcome and in need of a reason for almost everything.[5] It was Thomas who thought the disciples should die like Lazarus. Thomas was confused over where Jesus was going and would not believe in the resurrected Christ until he saw and touched Him.[6] In every instance, Jesus, with attention and courtesy, gave Thomas His time and eventually His proof. In response, Thomas gave Jesus his loyalty.

Nathanael (Bartholomew)

Nathanael brought a sense of special significance to the group of twelve. He was a man of the highest integrity with complete sincerity. There was no deceit in him. Jesus praised him for this and assured him of greater successes to come.

Nathanael was quiet, studious, and meditative. Unlike Thomas, he was the first to understand the true nature and significance of Jesus. He recognized and acknowledged Jesus as the Son of God. He had the vision to see that Jesus could bring about God's kingdom and the dedication to help Him in this higher spiritual purpose.

From the beginning, Jesus saw this in Nathanael and gave him His sympathy and may well have appropriately changed his name, Bartholomew, to Nathanael, meaning "gift of God."[7]

Simon

Simon the Zealot was a radical who strongly resisted Roman rule in Palestine. He supported his political cause with ruthless zeal in the service of God. A fanatic committed to righteous undertakings, he was a "do-gooder" to the point of becoming militant at times. Jesus accepted this and knew how to translate such anger into action.

Simon the Zealot, with his confrontive persuasion techniques, went against the conciliatory approach Jesus was teaching. But Jesus did not meet Simon on militant terms. Instead, we have every reason to believe that Jesus put aside His own self-importance, bridled the zeal, nurtured the self-esteem, and changed the political behavior of Simon, winning him over to promote God's kingdom.

Judas

Few will forget Judas Iscariot, the secretary-treasurer, who handled the administrative affairs and was the keeper of the money box. He had an extreme desire for wealth. Judas was accused by one of the disciples of embezzling funds. He betrayed Jesus to a company of high priests for a mere thirty pieces of silver. This was the priestly party that was to try to put Christ out of business.

Speculating on Judas' intentions in betraying Jesus is a complex endeavor. There are numerous motives suggested by biblical scholars, ranging from personal to political. The entire event is shrouded in mystery and sadness, but for our purposes here several popular conjectures will be presented.

Perhaps Judas realized there was a clash of purposes and wills between Jesus and the religious power structure. He had given three years of his life to Christ's mission, but things were not materializing the way he thought they should. He, like others of his day, was hoping for a political kingdom—one in which their Roman enemies would be crushed, the present evil conditions abolished, and the Jewish people redeemed.

When Jesus said He was leaving without launching a rebellion to usher in His political kingdom, Judas either out of greed or jealousy decided to sell Him out. He wanted to force Jesus to perform a miracle to bring about Judas' understanding of the kingdom.

Judas turned to back-room, back-stabbing, and bad-mouthing politics in making an "end run" around the head of his group. In the ultimate act of sabotage he betrayed his Master, precipitating Christ's death.

In short, Judas stopped serving those within his company. His thievery and betrayal of Jesus were at loggerheads with the cause of God's kingdom. He was living a life which focused only on self: self-interest, self-advancement, and self-satisfaction. He no longer supported the very reason for the disciples' being.

Jesus had identified Judas as the one who would betray Him. Jesus was fully aware of Judas' intentions. He did not interfere with Judas' actions, but did hold His betrayer accountable.[8] After his heinous deed Judas left, never to return as one of the twelve apostles. He was later replaced.

Judas is forever remembered as traitor and thief. Unfortunately he is more than a symbol. His kind may live on in any group of people organized together for a cause.

In examining the lives of a few disciples the key point to remember is that despite the many shortcomings of His management team—their diverse personalities, different appetites and ambitions, and internal disagreements—Jesus Christ molded and shaped this group of ordinary men into a "glorious company." They initiated and organized Christianity, which today is far and away the largest religion in the world. How did He do it? How did He combine a corporate mind and a servant heart?

His Corporate Culture (Beliefs and Behavior)

The corporate culture of Christ was built around concern for and care for others, not Himself. He immersed His self-regard and promoted humility of the heart. This gave Him an overwhelming and compelling appeal. This theme, putting your own self-importance aside and serving others, is the vital center of Jesus' teachings.

Jesus most clearly exemplified this belief by giving up His life for the sins of the world. His death on the cross served not only as a substitution for humankind, but as an example as well. Jesus' life and mission were aimed at directing people's focus away from themselves and toward others. According to Jesus, what most people struggle for—money, power, possessions, and recognition—are not really the true measurements of greatness. *In the kingdom of God, service to others is the true measurement of greatness.*

Jesus didn't use the "hard sell," bulldozing people into the kingdom, nor did He use the "soft sell," hoping to slyly influence. Rather He wooed and courted His listeners, never forgetting their needs. Jesus was a master teacher and trainer. He kept His pupils interested with parables that connected heaven with earth, involved by asking probing questions, and intrigued by sometimes even using silence to prod them to reveal their hidden thoughts.

Jesus Christ understood that self-motivation is to be cherished and nurtured among others, and He did just that. He challenged people to seek God's kingdom, and see the opportunity for greater spiritual happiness and success. He brought out the best in people by pulling (not pushing) them along.

Jesus had amazing control of His emotions. He turned away wrath with a soft answer, humored scornful criticism, and withstood violent accusations by saying nothing. Jesus was slow to anger. His patience—in explaining how there was a more rewarding way to think, work, and feel about everyday life—was inexhaustible. He worked hard at giving conciliatory arguments—ones that overcame distrust and hostility. But He was not always free from quarrels and disagreements; He could bring tough-minded, realistic thoughts to them when confronted.

Jesus got very angry when He saw businessmen (money changers) charging exorbitant prices to exchange currency for payment of the annual temple tax. They were exploiting the poor and making excessive profits in the name of religion. That gave religion a bad name. He called them hypocrites and crooks and personally stopped their dealings. It was always clear where Christ stood on such issues of kingdom business integrity.

Jesus, in the few times He got angry, did not direct it against an individual. It was always directed against attitudes, conditions, and groups. He directed His wrath against ideas and actions, but never people.

Like any leader with a sense of urgency to get the job done, He at times became impatient and irritated with His management team (the disciples). Do you not have eyes to see? Do you not have ears to listen? Are you as dull as the rest? He was bothered by their preoccupation with prominence and survival. They either could not understand or failed to manage the issue at hand—which was service for the benefit of others.

He never supported political behavior where people used power, cunningness, or deceit to shade the truth or attack others from their "blind side." He had no time for what is often referred to as office politics in this day and time. He was a servant leader who led by placing others first. Jesus managed His personal relationships openly and honestly. And He demanded the same of His apostles.

He was both a positive thinker and doer. His thoughts and words were solution-oriented, not problem-prone. He changed the Golden Rule of that day from "What you hate, do not do to anyone" to "Do to others what you would have them do to you."[9]

Unlike His peers, He developed intimate associations with those with whom He worked. He called people from all social and economic backgrounds, developing their sense of self-worth and their value to each other and God's world.

Finally, unlike other teachers of His day, He actively associated women with His mission. He rejected the traditional attitude that they were inferior to men by nature because they had been created only secondhand, out of the substance of man.

At a time when women were classed with slaves, heathen, and brutish men, Christ welcomed them and had many female followers. They included Mary, Joanna, and Susanna. At a time when His peers forbade women to study religion and debated the existence of the female soul, Jesus taught women frequently. The Lord even commended Mary for staying out of the kitchen and listening to what He said.[10] Throughout His life and after His death, these female followers were conspicuously faithful to Jesus.

His Management Style

Jesus Christ, in His time and age, exhibited the best qualities of the classic general management styles prevalent in American business today. He was a "company man" who identified the success of His life and mission with His obedience to the Father's will. He had a strong concern for the human side of His company of followers. He was dedicated to the highest quality of integrity—ethically, morally, and spiritually.

All these gave the apostles a stronger meaning and motivation to carry out His mission.

Jesus did not lord it over others. Unlike His priestly peers, He did not display His authority by strutting about the marketplace in fine flowing robes or by seeking the seats of prominence at public functions and private dinner parties. Jesus' authority resided in Him, not from the trappings of success around Him. He had little money, few possessions, and no title or power position.

Jesus did not hesitate to use His authority when it was in the best interests of His mission. In dealing with people, He never let unethical conduct go unchecked, poor performance unnoticed, or lack of accountability unanswered. He addressed them directly and openly, but always supported and encouraged a change of heart for the person involved. He showed that the way to repentance was marked by forgiveness.

Jesus had some of the best qualities of the "gamesman" style of management as described by Michael Maccoby in *The Gamesman: The New Corporate Leaders*, "He enjoyed new ideas, new techniques, fresh approaches and shortcuts." This is evident from His innovative teaching style marked by insightful sayings and parables. "The contest hyped Him up and He communicated His enthusiasm, thus energizing others. His talk and His thinking were terse, dynamic, sometimes playful, and in quick flashes."[11]

He took risks. He left the safety of Capernaum to go to the danger of Jerusalem. He confronted the authority of the Pharisees and the teachings of the scribes. He placed His mission in the hands of twelve ordinary men. But unlike many of the gamesmen in the management ranks of companies today, Jesus was not out to prove Himself a winner. He was out to allow others to be victorious, if they participated in His kingdom.

He refused to practice a Machiavellian style of management where the goal is power to enhance the chances of succeeding. Jesus didn't see His peers as enemies to be confronted in "win-lose situations." Nor did He see the disciples as objects to be manipulated for His success, but rather as human beings to be inspired for the greater good of God's kingdom.

He stressed and exemplified teamwork, promoting a spirit of cooperation, not competitive individualism among the apostles. He would not allow any "we/they" barriers. At the same time He recognized people's driving instincts to achieve personal success and greatness in their work. He promoted a spirited competition among the disciples, but not the kind where one jockeys for position or undercuts others to get ahead. Rather, He promoted competition against a standard of excellence to achieve fullness of life.

Thus His disciples, men of different but special talents, were able to accomplish far more together, unified by a kingdom cause, than as individuals working against one another.

His Strongest Management Trait

There were numerous instances in Jesus' ministry when He could have compromised His mission and become a hero or earthly king to His followers. The people were looking for a messianic political king. Jesus knew He was a spiritual king. His mission at that point was not to be an earthly ruler.

With respect to His human nature, we can see that He could have easily become captivated by His early successes at Capernaum and begun to think too highly of His own power. He could have let His pride and ego cause Him to trust and promote only Himself. He could have said, "My human achievements are sufficient for Me." Of course, He didn't do that. He remained faithful to His Heavenly Father's mission. Jesus' style of leadership was humble—not heroic.

Jesus has recently been called a "man for others" and plentiful is the evidence that He did not use His miraculous powers to obtain power, honor, or glory. In fact, Jesus was without pretense, show, or thought of reward. He lived a life consistent with what He taught. J.B. Phillips' translation of

Jesus' words accurately captures the nuances of His teachings in parlance that fits our concerns here:

> The only "superior" among you is the one who serves others. For every man who promotes himself will be humbled and every man who learns to be humble will find promotion.
>
> Everyone who sets himself as somebody will become a nobody, and the man who makes himself nobody will become somebody.[12]

If there was one modern management trait that carried Jesus Christ from a nobody to a somebody, it was His service to and for the benefit of others—His *servant leadership*.

From a human perspective Jesus seemed to fail in the short term, but from the divine perspective, He greatly succeeded in the short and long term. He won the crown of glory and honor. And He didn't do it through physical or economic power, or through intellectual or political achievements. He did it through the hearts of men and women by giving Himself to others.

FIVE

Servant Leadership:
Management at Its Best

Christ's strongest leadership trait, His servant attitude, shows us a way to manage and motivate people to willing action by helping them become all they were created to be in reaching their fullest potential. It is management at its best, and it can easily be translated into today's business world.

Managers should view themselves as *developers of people*, not as *"take charge"* heroes. They should help others thrive and flourish, and in doing so they themselves will succeed to their utmost. *Servant leadership* does not mean taking a subservient role. It is not weak and submissive as the name may imply. Rather, it is cultivating a supportive role that puts self-serving interests and ego gratification aside with the goal of serving the development needs of others. Practicing *servant leadership* does not mean that you cast aside personal ambition and career goals. It recognizes the "driving instinct" in people to want to achieve personal success and greatness in their work.

But remember, ambition is healthy only when worthwhile goals are achieved, not at the expense of, but with the help of others. Ambition is the most mature, "not when we know what we want and how to get it, but when we understand what we possess and how to give it."[1] It is the most meaningful and virtuous when it is for the benefit of others.

Servant leadership does not abolish the necessary demands a good manager must place upon others, such as competency, obedience, discipline, excellence, and hard work. It does bring an added dimension to effective management. *Servant leadership* gets close to the heart of the matter. It combines a servant heart—softness, feeling, and generosity, with a corporate mind—tough-minded, realistic thought.

Its keystone is concern for others—and communicating this attitude through actions that say, "I'm for you." The Apostle Paul's instructions sum up the *servant leadership* message: you must see others as worthy of preferential treatment.

It is management's dedication to this higher spiritual purpose that brings a sense of special significance to the workplace and inspires and enlists the devotion of people. It is the "high touch" aspect of servant leadership that breeds quality productivity in people and makes for effective management. And it is through this concern for others that management can make its greatest contribution to the growth of people, and in turn the development of a business in succeeding.

Feelings are the *most powerful* human motivators, not pay raises, not a title on the door and a carpet on the floor, not a corner office, not fabulous fringe benefits—but feelings. Feelings are the driving force behind us all, upon which we either live our lives happily and productively or sadly and unfruitfully. Various independent research studies verify the crucial role that feelings play.[2]

Experts tell us that humans use less than thirty percent of their mental potential.[3] (In fact, an examination after death would reveal millions of underdeveloped brain cells.) Why? Too often people fail to achieve their "ideal best." This occurs because their potential is not fully developed in their personal lives or in their work world. These shortcomings cause them to become hurt and negative; their highest productivity is lost.

No matter what your position, executive, middle manager, team leader, or individual midst peers, the questions are the same. What do you do to change this? And how do you go about it?

Nurture Their Nature

How can you motivate people to reach their potential? You nurture their nature—their human nature. Begin this by enhancing their feelings. Make them feel good about themselves, their work, and others. Cultivate their closeness. Promote their support. Nourish their self-esteem. Feed them recognition. Show people that not only their work counts, but they count as well. In short, you satisfy the two most pressing human needs in the workplace: "the need to be wanted and the need to be needed."

This creates positive feelings. Positive feelings are like antibodies that neutralize stress, open up the mind for innovation, and motivate for increased productivity. They encourage rich relationships rather than competitive individualism. They create a trusting atmosphere that builds loyalty among the team members and to their leader. The results are growth for the individual, the company, and you. All of this leads to a key insight. Remember, the "human" nature of people: *they want to know how much you care before they care how much you know.*

One of the most remarkable examples of nurture is the caring relationship between the hummingbird and a group of unusual plants. We can learn much from it.

Though it is the smallest of all warm-blooded animals, it

has the biggest heart—relative to its size. This big heart allows it to be most productive. It can feed on as many as 1,000 flowers a day and fly up to 500 miles nonstop. It can fly backwards, sideways, and even lift itself straight up and hover like a helicopter. No other bird has all these abilities.

It is highly adaptable to different situations in its life. It can live productively in environments ranging from 100°F. to subzero temperatures, from the warm desert to the harsh Andes.

The hummingbird's primary source of food is nectar. There is a select group of flowers that only attract and provide nectar for hummingbirds. Their blooms are red and easily seen, often tubular, hanging horizontally or in pendant fashion, and suitable only to the long bill of the hummingbird. They grow wide apart so there is no danger of the fragile hummingbird becoming entangled; they have no appendages to attract insects and other birds while the hummingbird is feeding.

These flowers have developed a nectar specially for the hummingbird. The nectar is liquid, has just the right sugar level, and can be easily sipped. These unique flowers also provide unusually soft and delicate filaments inside their blooms to cover and protect the very fragile eggs in the hummingbird's nest.

Because of the unique design of these flowers, they depend solely on the hummingbird for pollination. But a young hummingbird does not instinctively know it should visit these flowers. It is a learned process. Slowly, through trial and error, the hummingbird learns that these flowers are the source of greatest satisfaction and essential for survival.

As it responds, darting from blossom to blossom, it pulls out the deep riches within, caressing the petals with its wings. In doing so, it gets pollen on its crown, throat, and chin and transports it to other flowers of the same species. The result is often pollination and more of the beautiful blossoms from which the hummingbird can refresh itself again and again.

Truly, the hummingbird is a servant to these flowers, helping them thrive and flourish, and in being so, sustains its own growth and development as one of God's most beautiful and talented creatures.[4]

The "Commandments of Caring"

What follows in succeeding chapters are ways to nurture the human nature, help others thrive and flourish, and sustain your own growth and development. They are called the "commandments of caring" and are patterned upon the ways Christ successfully managed and motivated people. To be effective, they have to be practiced with absolute honesty—every day, every way—in everything you do and say. Break the bond of trust with false pretenses only once and you could destroy your credibility forever.

These "commandments of caring" may or may not adapt easily into your management style. But work at using them, as hard as you work at understanding the technicalities of the business. The contradiction between the effects of an unhealthy ambition—selfishness, hostility, envy, and greed—and Christian values are resolved through a godly approach, not a magic managerial solution. Such resolution can lead to greater spiritual development for all those involved.

God's authority is over all of His creation. His truth applies to all of life. Jesus is Lord not only over the church, home, and family, but He is Lord over the marketplace as well. His teachings are as relevant to twentieth-century Park Avenue as they were to first-century Palestine. Through the "commandments of caring," you can, like Christ, promote and exemplify *servant leadership*. You can learn to integrate your faith into your work and take another step in the Christian journey. The Saviour of Sunday morning wants to be Lord of your workweek. The "commandments of caring" provide a way to follow in His paths.

PART THREE

Making the Approach Work: "The Commandments of Caring"

Judge First with Your Heart, Not Your Head

Feelings can make or break us. A sociologist's research on National Merit Scholarship finalists demonstrates this crucial truth. Working with the brightest kids in the country, from all walks of life, he wanted to discover the common denominator among them. The results of his study are revealing. He gave his report on a 3″ x 5″ card as follows: "There seems to be only one thing common to all these extraordinary students. Somebody in the past made them *feel* infinitely important."

Every person has feelings, from the ones that sweep the factory floor and clean the office urinals to the ones that occupy the executive suites, from those who report to you to those who are across the hall trying to get ahead of you. Feelings are the bridge of communication that link us all. Everything you say to or do with a person helps him or her develop and shows that person whether you really care. As a manager, you need to be aware what certain "signs" may reveal to your workers:

- the expression on your face;
- the tone of your voice;
- your eye contact with them;
- the movement of your fingertips;
- your attention span;
- the courtesies you extend.

All of these signs communicate something important to others. They hold the power to discourage or elevate a worker. When you give someone your time and attention, you are practicing the theme of this book: the belief that all people have an inherent value by virtue of being created in the image of God and thus an inherent right to develop to their fullest potential. This attitude can only be sustained by *judging first with your heart, not your head.* You must show concern for the developmental needs of your employees. This is the first commandment of caring.

It is important that you not only want to help people develop, but that you want to see them succeed as well. Too often, a manager says, "I want her to succeed," while really feeling, "I wish her well, but I don't want her to do better than me." This falls short of the ideal.

This first commandment of caring is not intended to ignore the judging of competency. As a manager or project leader, you still recognize and reward superior management skills and accomplishments when substantiated by positive proof. This is the "left brain," rational approach that belongs with the "tough-minded, realistic thought" side of performance evaluations.

The first commandment says that in developing and motivating others to succeed, you must lead with sincere feelings, setting your own importance aside and saying, "I want to see people succeed. I am going to help people develop." This shows people that you care about them. Ultimately, this is what enlists their devotion. This is Christian love in practice and it pulls (not pushes) people to do bigger and better things.

Love is a word which we as business people, even as Christians, sometimes find hard to define in the workplace. If we are even able to grasp what love means, we are even less likely to adequately practice it. Let's face it, we are uncomfortable with expressing love in the work world. The trouble lies in our culture's popular definition of love as a spontaneous natural affection in which emotion plays the prominent role and over which we have little or no control. True Christian love—*agape*—is not marked by sentimental sappiness but by a deliberate decision. *Agape* love is expressed by actions where the entire personality, especially the will, is involved. It is not necessarily marked by a display of emotions. It is a matter of commitment, covenant, and promise.

Managers who hold feelings back from their people are not always emotionally dead. Their inability to express what is inside them doesn't mean they don't feel things. Perhaps they feel as deeply as the more expressive manager. The visible and genuine actions of nonexpressive managers can still convey deep concerns and warm feelings. We need to recognize and respect this form of Christian love in our business relationships. But for those who tend to be more reserved, they need to go the second mile in making sure that their concern comes across as genuine and visible.

When Jesus reinstated Peter, He asked Peter three successive times if he loved Him. He surely wasn't demanding or pressuring for an emotional response each time from Peter, but was testing to see if Peter's entire personality, including his will, was involved. Peter's answer was "Yes, Lord." The Lord's final reply then was, "Feed My sheep."[1] And Peter went out and did exactly that in his ministry.

For those managers (and companies) committed to helping others to develop as a mission of their management philosophy, it is the first step in building a trusting and binding relationship with their people. In order to succeed, however, you have to do more than just talk the talk. The walk begins with action. As Robert Waterman reminds us in *The Renewal Factor*, "Action may start with words, but it has to be backed by symbolic action that makes those words come alive ... the most up-to-date personnel policies are moot in comparison with the power of a manager's attitudes and his visible attention."[2]

SEVEN

Excite with Enthusiasm

The word enthusiasm comes from the Greek word *entheos*, meaning "God within." Christ was truly "God within" human flesh. His works were for the glory of God. This was the focus of His proclamation, and He fervently developed His message as an opportunity to involve others. It was an inspiring vision for His followers, and it motivated them to achieve far beyond their abilities.

Excite with enthusiasm. This is the second commandment of caring. Build your enthusiasm on the foundation of "God within" you. Use this as a springboard to motivate others. This is what excites people. They long to be part of a vision. This is what makes ordinary people do extraordinary things.

Mary Kay Ash, founder and Chairman Emeritus, Mary Kay Cosmetics, Inc., is a splendid example. She instills a "people management" philosophy in her company, built on the Golden Rule. In Mary Kay Cosmetics, "p & l" does not mean profit and loss—it means people and love. She built a company that has achieved annual sales exceeding $300 million and a net income of $130 million by using more than 200,000 women in an "enthusiastic, well-trained, and motivated sales organization." She says, "A record such as this could never have been accomplished without the enthusiasm of thousands of women." And she built that enthusiasm "through a sensitivity for the needs of others" and by offering women an unlimited opportunity for success.[1]

Don't build your enthusiasm on theatrics to impress others and serve your own needs. If you do, your play will close down in a few days. If you build your enthusiasm on something that does not involve the "blooming of others," it will eventually wither in the eyes of others. It will be like my eighty-eight-year-old friend (she has the spirit of a thirty-year-old) experienced. Her eyes are so bad that she mistook super phosphate for lime and put it on everything in her garden. She said, "Everything just shot up and died!"

When you are consumed with sincere enthusiasm, those around you cannot help but respond in kind. I've seen it turn a pessimist into an optimist, laziness into productiveness, and weak into record sales. But if you don't show it, people won't know it. We've all seen the moving effects of the "rah-rah for our team" approach at company functions, stirred up by songs, music, or a motivational speaker. They are moving, but just for the moment.

Enthusiasm doesn't have to be shouted. It can be quiet and most effective. The most meaningful, enduring, and exciting enthusiasm is that of a manager showing it in one-on-one relationships—when the recipient (not a speaker) is on center stage. It can be shown in simple ways: the spring in your step as you come from your desk to greet that person (which says I'm glad to be with you again); the grin on your face (which says I have good feelings about you); the wink of an eye (that says you're someone special), or the firm handshake with both hands (that says you deserve special attention). These expressions of caring produce confidence in people and gives them the feeling that they are destined for something special.

Another way of exciting people is to present them with the opportunity to take on a challenging project. Perhaps you might suggest one that they can help create. People tend to support what they help to develop. Here, though, the manager goes at it a little differently, as Edwin H. Land, founder of Polaroid, suggests, "The first thing you naturally do is to teach the person to feel that the undertaking is manifestly important and nearly impossible. That draws out the kind of drives that make people strong."[2] His suggestion is an excellent example of how to motivate your workers with an inspiring vision.

"Cardboard" Enthusiasm Isn't the Answer

Genuine and dedicated enthusiasm is not achieved through a management declaration expressed or solicited through wall slogans or posters. It begins with expressing an opportunity for people.

A technically brilliant, machine-oriented, chief executive of a large company got excited when he heard a talk about industrial perfection. He was eager to energize the rest of the company and immediately ordered that signs, bearing the word PERFECTION, be placed throughout the offices and factories. Subordinates scurried, artists hurried, and the print shop worked late. In a very short period the signs were everywhere, in all shapes and sizes, on office desks, hallway walls, factory machines, and conference and dining room tables.

It caused a lot of curiosity, a lot of talk, a lot of lip service, but little genuine excitement. Sure, most everyone knew what was trying to be done, but no one solicited employees in specific areas for their ideas or told them of their opportunities in striving for perfection. This CEO understood the nature of machines, but not the nature of people. His project succeeded with machines, but failed with people.

I've seen some of the most capable managers fail to reach their potential because of a lack of enthusiasm. They simply could not get the strong, aggressive support of their people. I've seen great business concepts and ideas die. There was no "feeling" promoting them, and they never caught the interest and attention of upper management.

If you have enthusiasm, thank God for it. If you don't, ask God for it. Practice it, develop it, and do it in a Christian way: *make it an opportunity to involve others.*

EIGHT

Socialize, Don't Ostracize

to banish or exclude from a group

"I would rather be laughed at than ignored. I am grateful for the amount of attention I attract."[1] These are the words of Michael Anderson, a midget. His comment illustrates the deep-seated human need to be recognized. It is a pressing human need.

Christ's ministry filled this need in people. He went out of His way to make people feel part of a community where they were important to each other. He ate, talked, walked, and prayed with the apostles. He mingled among the common people. He talked with and touched lepers.

You as a manager (or mentor) can meet that need in others by using one of the most effective but neglected forms of ministry in business. *Socialize with the people you supervise in a casual, relaxed atmosphere.* Break down the barriers of aloofness. Get to know them better, their family

69

backgrounds, and their outside interests. Understand their job problems, skills, and career aspirations. There is something about a casual, relaxed atmosphere of open expression that creates a closer bond between people. This is the third rule for caring managers. This type of socializing creates a community of interests and a desire to support one another and do good work to show that support.

Have you heard the "amazing maze" story? Once upon a time there were two mice in an experimental maze. One of the two was larger and more experienced in medical research than the other. Each, though, wandered for days trying to find a way out of the network of blind alleys. They had "walls of aloofness" between them. One day they met each other over a piece of cheese and began talking. They found they had formerly worked in the same laboratory and under the same boss—whom they both admired. After discovering they had similar tastes in cheeses, they talked about the long hours and hard demands of being a laboratory mouse. They began to talk about their current project. Discussing how to get out of the maze, they soon had the problem worked out. The larger, more experienced mouse supported his smaller friend on his shoulders and then stood up, lifting him high so he could see above the walls of the maze and find their way out. The two mice won much praise for their ingenuity, the finest gourmet cheeses for their feat, and a prize for the medical research team.

This farcical anecdote illustrates the benefits that emerge during socializing. The socialization time led to a spirit of cooperation and eventually the solution to the problem.

Take Time to Socialize

Too many managers say they don't have the time to socialize and to create a community feeling among their people. It does take time, but it saves time, with the increased productivity and loyalty gained more than covering your small investment of time.

Often managers say, "I'm not trying to win any popularity

contests. Nice guys finish last. I don't care if my people like me as long as they respect me." Such thinking is distorted. Most people will give much more effort to please someone they both like and respect.

J. Robert McGuff heads up Blue Cross and Blue Shield of Tennessee, the state's largest health care insurer. He has completed forty years of service with the company, yet still likes to begin each day in the company cafeteria having coffee with his associates. One of his workers has this to say, "People feel more comfortable when they see the boss having coffee in the cafeteria rather than behind the locked doors of his office. It makes him more approachable."[2]

Mike Quinlan, CEO at McDonald's Corporation, the fast-food giant that continues to widen its sales lead in the industry, goes out of his way to be one of the guys. For business lunches he often chooses a local place with a relaxed atmosphere rather than a formal "uptown" restaurant. Sometimes he calls his managers together for impromptu meetings at the McDonald's restaurant on the ground floor of the headquarters building. At company picnics, he willingly participates in carnival games, even allowing himself to be dunked in a tank of water. He goes out of his way to socially accept others and to be socially acceptable.[3]

There are obvious ways to create a casual atmosphere outside of the office—lunchtime, dinner in your home, or the golf course. But you have to struggle with it at work to make it work. It begins with junking the agenda and juggling your planned work schedule for your office that day.

Back in the office, practice "management by wandering around." Begin by walking into one of your employee's office (versus asking them into yours). The fact that you, the manager, takes time to come to that employee will make that person feel good. Be sure you let the other person do the talking. Most people are hungry to talk about themselves. For those few who are not, use the "pregnant pause," that is, after you have cued a topic of their interest, pause in silence for a period of time. This will usually encourage the stubbornest or shiest person to speak.

Never shut your office door. It does nothing but get people uptight, create suspicion, and encourage rumors. It is interesting to note that no McDonald's employee, the CEO included, at the company's headquarters has an office door. The only private place on the executive floor is a circular conference room.

As you "manage by wandering around," don't play the role of a company guardian by checking up on people. I'm reminded of the technically brilliant, but arrogant management style of a chief executive officer I once knew. When he made his daily rounds on the factory floors, he meddled to the point of becoming the laughingstock of the employees.

He eventually reaped his just rewards. As he bristled through the factory one morning, he noticed a worker relaxing by the Coke machine. As he passed by the worker he addressed a scowling look toward him, obviously perturbed with the lack of productivity. Twenty minutes later he passed the same relaxing worker again and furiously confronted him saying, "I've had it; you've had it. No one in my company is going to take that long a break. You're fired, and don't think I can't do that!"

The worker paused, smiled, and said: "Nope, I don't think you can, because I work for the Coca-Cola Company."

Sharing Is Socializing

Ken Sargent, President of Alan Bates Corporation, a health care system, relates a very successful "coffee and commitment" approach to socializing:

> When I was a middle manager, our group met for coffee every morning, with no exceptions, for ten minutes. Each of us took one minute to share two things: something he knew was happening in the hospital that day and something he intended to do that day. We didn't discuss implications; we just shared and ended by shaking hands. The pressure

to meet the needs of either top management or those in our departments was immense—we met anyway. Our meetings were simple, but powerful: we knew what was happening everywhere in the hospital, we understood what each of us was trying to do, and we were committed to each other.[4]

Then there is the "how not to do it" version of this approach which I saw firsthand. I call it "coffee and colonialism." It was designed to be a morning meeting where the senior management of the company had coffee together. The most senior manager had control of the meeting. It was held in his office with managers sitting around his desk, drinking coffee (which they paid for) out of his specially built alcove of refreshments. His attitude was usually negative and his temperament foul. His silent motto had to be, "The glass is always half empty," and as one officer added, "The water always stale."

It was nonparticipatory management at its worst. The executive dominated the conversation and had full control of all thoughts and words spoken. He was the only person I ever knew who edited other people's dialogue. He was difficult to interrupt, and if you had a comment, he either added to it, ignored it, or put you down. Managers would keep looking for holes in the conversation, but he left few openings. The result was that people withdrew, didn't bring their best ideas forward, and failed to share other problems.

Such a hostile management-dominated approach transforms what could be a casual and productive atmosphere into a tense, uptight, and nonproductive meeting. It creates barriers of trust, and destroys opportunities for developing a community of interests and closer bond between people. In short, it makes no one feel needed.

As managers, we need to recognize people and make them feel a part of something. This requires authentic socializing and spending quality time with those we lead and influence. Like Jesus, we must share ourselves with others.

NINE

Understand People That Differ from You

In meeting people we too often judge them based on "the ten second impression" (as it is called in the executive search business), and proceed to label them positively or negatively confirming our intuitive appraisal. Other times, as we work with people, we often find that they don't mirror the company's image in the way they look, manage, or live. Since their ideas don't agree with ours, we decide that they don't fit in.

I have already noted the motley crew that made up Jesus' disciples. The fact that He was able to transform this ragtag team into faithful followers is a tribute to His strategizing. Jesus opened opportunities for others with different ideas than His. He refused to reject those who did not initially fit in. Such rejection frequently occurs in boss/subordinate relationships when a new supervisor or regime of management moves into place. Boss/subordinate is the perspective, if not the words, of the new management. With this attitude in control the "squeeze" in the relationship begins, with the boss trying to squeeze the employee into his image. Often, particularly if the subordinate is doing a good job, and the boss cannot accept the employee's beliefs or management style, then the squeezing starts in the area of externals or incidentals. One manager tells this story:

> I was just getting ready to leave the company's apartment in New York for the evening, when one of the company's senior executives, a friend of mine, walked in and asked if I had a few minutes. He was my sponsor, and we shared many of the same beliefs and values about business and the managing of people. He had a few social drinks and mustered up the courage to pass on some things about me that bothered the CEO, his boss. The next ten minutes centered on a blue suit I wore (and had on at that time), that according to the CEO, "looks like it came off the back of a U.S. postal worker." I was half-mad, half-amused. I was mad because after all those years, this CEO had never bothered to give me (or anyone else) a performance review—but he was willing to evaluate my dress. I was amused because the suit was of the finest English wool, classic in its styling and appearance, and tailored like those in the finest shops on Savile Row in London. I almost wondered aloud, "He wears his Gucci belt buckle, watch, and shoes to the boardroom, why can't I wear my English suit in the hallways?"

A year later this manager was dismissed with the statement, "This has nothing to do with your work. You have done a good job. You just don't fit in."

Frequently you read in the *Wall Street Journal* about a

management group being replaced because they didn't fit in. In one case, without any business justification, I saw a new regime gain a "power foothold" and oust more than a dozen officers whose combined experience in that industry approached 200 years. Over the years the stockholders had invested millions of dollars in the development of these officers. These executives who had played a major role in making and keeping the company an industry leader were asked to find another job or "rewarded" with early retirement.

The new regime pressed for doing postaudits on capital expenditures projects and measuring return on assets; it was like a "report card" according to one executive. The new management didn't consider people to be an asset, because if they had, they would have realized they were decimating the return on millions of dollars invested in the development of those officers they characterized as "not fitting in." They made little attempt to evaluate the prior accomplishments and character of these officers. Instead, they simply concluded that this group was incompatible.

We can learn an important lesson from this incident. We, as managers, must beware of the temptation to evaluate people based on externals and incidentals and not by native worth. *Understand people that differ from you.* This is a crucial commandment of caring.

Interdependence, Not Intolerance

Japanese management base their personnel relationships on interdependence, not intolerance. "Peers, superiors and subordinates provide support and assistance to one another, and they depend on one another even when they pretend otherwise."[1] Interdependence builds deep human relationships, unifying individuals through the stresses and joys of achieving company goals. Intolerance, which creates the inability to hear and understand people with ideas that differ from yours, makes for an unhealthy competitiveness and pollutes teamwork.

The wisest manager of men and women had this to say,

"Pay attention to what you hear. What you get depends on what you give. What you give you will get back, only more so."[2] You will find, more often than not, that with such an approach of interdependence and tolerance, not only will your business relationships survive, they will thrive.

In the real world there will be times when you try to listen to and understand people with different ideas, yet when you give much in doing this you will get back nothing but grief.

Can you ever be sure who to trust? Consider the story of the scorpion and the turtle:

> A scorpion, being a very poor swimmer, asked a turtle to carry him on his back across a river. "Are you mad?" exclaimed the turtle. "You'll sting me while I'm swimming, and I'll drown."
>
> "My dear turtle," laughed the scorpion, "if I were to sting you, you would drown, and I would go down with you. Now where is the logic in that?"
>
> "You're right!" cried the turtle. "Hop on!" The scorpion climbed aboard and halfway across the river gave the turtle a mighty sting. As they both sank to the bottom, the turtle said, "Do you mind if I ask you something? You said there'd be no logic in you stinging me. Why did you do it?"
>
> "It has nothing to do with logic," the drowning scorpion sadly replied, "it's just my character."[3]

The moral of the story is to be careful. The business world is filled with scorpions. Rarely will you encounter people who think exactly like you. The good news is that God is in control, and He will work in our lives through other people. As a chief executive officer of a large and successful company reminds us, "God has chosen many different people and circumstances to break, mold, and develop me and the most exciting thing about the process is that it is continuing."[4]

TEN
Support Your People

support(sə-pôrt, -pōrt) tr. v. -ported, -porting, -ports. 1. To bear the weight of, esp. from below. 2. To hold in position so as to keep from falling, sinking, or slipping. 3. To be capable of bearing: withstand. 4. To keep from failing or yielding from stress.[1]

A main function of any manager is offering support to his or her employees. When do you support your staff? The answer is always:

- When their sales are down—support them.
- When their efficiency is down—support them.
- When their quality is down—support them.
- When their production is down—support them.
- When they fail in a new venture—support them.

Keep involved with your workers. If a project turns out poorly, find some way to share the blame. Don't second guess and criticize after an outcome is known. Hindsight is always 20/20 vision. Instead, help them to try it again. Remove the fear of failure.

Don't allow relationships with people who make "end runs" around their management to undermine the responsible person or group under pressure. We don't need "Judas" types in the workplace. Support the person or people accountable, not office politics.

The giant sequoia tree dramatizes the importance of managers supporting their people, particularly at critical points in their careers. Sequoia trees grow to be hundreds of feet tall and live for thousands of years. With this great height and long life, you would think they would have deep roots. They don't. Sequoias stand together in a grove with wide ranging roots that closely interweave with one another. It is this mutual support that gives the trees stability during the harshest weather. The trees don't just take from their environment; they also give. They provide shelter and nutrition to neighboring plants and animals. The sequoia contributes 80 percent more to the forest environment than it takes. It drops its branches and needles, enriching the environment in which it lives by feeding other life.[2]

Sequoias never stop growing, but always support one another and continue to contribute to their immediate environment. No doubt that's why they are so respected and live so long.

The Times They Need You Most
Psychologists tell us there are four critical times in a person's career cycle when close support from others is desperately needed:

1. when we are first hired, promoted, or moved into a new position and trying to get the "lay of the land" and how to cultivate it;

2. during the middle management phase when we are seeking to make it big;
3. in mid-life crisis when we lose our precious youth and often say, "Is that all there is after working so hard all these years?"
4. when we are forced to resign or are fired from a job.[3]

Don Moers, Director of People Services in ServiceMaster's southeast area, has developed an effective way of managing those times when a person moves into a new position and needs that "somebody out there cares for me" support. He describes it as "nonthreatening third-party support."

He makes it a point to telephone the person two to four times in the first year of new assignment, asking such questions as: "How are you doing? How is the new job? Is the move working out?" He seeks to open the door to talk freely about the positives and negatives of the job, even when it involves personality conflicts. He also wants to insure newly hired employees have chosen the right company.[4]

Don's approach provides a "sounding board" for the new assignee to work out any frustrations. He then lubricates those situations where there is friction between people and offers advice on how to resolve problems and take advantage of opportunities. This is called supporting your people, and it is done at a time when they need it most.

One of the most stressful times often overlooked by management is the mid-life crisis. The following story tragically illustrates the results of such neglect.

Dave, a longtime and productive employee, had worked his way up to become an officer in a newly formed holding company of a conglomerate. Shortly thereafter, at the age of forty-five, he began to display some of the symptoms of a mid-life crisis. Troubles at home and a carefree lifestyle outside the office led to problems in his work efficiency. Rather than recognizing Dave's symptoms, his superiors allowed him to slide. A younger, highly ambitious junior executive, hired and trusted by Dave, seized the opportunity, promoted his own ego, and maneuvered to take over Dave's position. Embarrassed, Dave was eventually forced to resign. Humiliated, he became bitterly depressed and shortly thereafter was diagnosed as having a terminal disease. In the weeks before Dave's death he refused to see anyone. He died a most unhappy man.

A friend of Dave's had this to say, "They kicked him when he was down. They may not have pulled the trigger, but they pointed the gun. How unfeeling can people be?"

How many more stories like this one are there in American business where support of management and peers could have made a positive and lasting difference in a person's life? Christ made the difference in Peter's life by supporting him in his most critical crisis. You can make a difference in people's lives by supporting them when they need you most.

With support, people can manage stressful pressures. Without it, they can be destroyed. A personal effort of expression on your part, a face-to-face meeting, a phone call, or a sincere note can make a positive and lasting difference in a person's life and for the company. *Support your people when they need you most.* This is the fifth command followed by caring managers.

One day I sat by a stranger for lunch in a crowded deli. He was Vietnamese, worked with computers, and had just gotten back from a vacation with his mother and brother on the West Coast. He obviously wanted to be with them, mentioning he had tried for thirteen years to get a transfer to San Jose. I suggested that he wouldn't have any problem finding a job in that area with his computer experience.

"Oh, no," he said, "I would never leave IBM; my supervisor has been too good to me. My family and I had tried for years to get my father out of Communist Vietnam, but when we finally could, he was too old and frail to travel. The day he died, my supervisor, who unbeknownst to me had been staying close to this situation, talked to me and suggested I take off from work and come back when I felt like it." My luncheon companion ended his story with, "Right now IBM is cutting costs to meet foreign competition on the smaller computers. Maybe later, when things get better, I can get a transfer."

An employee of ServiceMaster tells a similar story about her ups and downs. She had just gained a small new customer in a tiny town in Alabama. The president of the division called and congratulated her. Her comment: "That's as good as a bonus."

Later in her career she was removed from her assignment after only two and one-half months, due to a political situation beyond her control. Stunned and bitter, she considered other employment options. Again, top management offered support, first by giving her an interview with the vice president of operations. Then later, by periodic phone calls of encouragement while she was temporarily traveling, they let her know that they were still working to find her an assignment. She remains today with ServiceMaster in a higher position, more committed than ever.

These are illustrations of the type of support management must offer. Such meaningful gestures of assistance were not soon forgotten. In the long run, they paid off in benefits for both the individual and the companies.

Sincerity Counts
Seemingly small amounts of sincere support, given at the right time, can make an important difference in the development of a person. A perceptive manager looks for and promotes these opportunities.

Take, for example, the case of a young woman who had just become the first female brand manager in the marketing department of a *Fortune* 100 company. She had been in the job only a few weeks when she was requested to make a brand review presentation before the board of directors. She was frightened by the prospect, but grew even more terrified as she sat in the boardroom waiting for her turn. At a coffee break just before she was to go on, the CEO walked over to her and whispered in her ear, "Remember, Ellen, you know more about this brand's marketing strengths and weaknesses than anyone in this room." She did know more, and she went on to make an excellent presentation. Later, she became a senior executive in the company and to this day credits the CEO's help as a turning point in her development.

Trivial, meaningless situations—you may say—but not in the minds of the people who experienced them. Such moments of caring can become the turning points in people's lives.

Your support of people has to have a genuine feeling behind it. It cannot be manipulative or a "trick of the trade." A close friend describes a glaring situation he experienced where the support lacked authentic sentiment:

> The new president of a conglomerate I worked for followed the practice of sending birthday cards to the officers of the major subsidiary companies. Thus, the very day I was told to resign from the company, which coincided with my birthday, I received a card in my home mail saying, "May I wish you a happy birthday and continued success," signed by the president who wanted me out. With some inquiry I discovered what happened. The president had his secretary buy birthday cards at the first of each year and he signed them all at one time. His secretary then got the birth dates from the personnel department, and as these dates popped up in her suspense file, she sent the cards out. The president had failed to update his secretary on my leaving the company. Several years later when this man was told by his board of directors to retire early, I had to resist the temptation to send him a card on his birthday that said, "May I wish you a happy birthday and continued success."

The Great Jackass Fallacy

The alternative to supporting and encouraging people, and it is practiced more than one might think, is to motivate by reward and punishment—the carrot-and-stick philosophy. If you succeed you get rewarded with a carrot; if you fail you get punished with a stick. The management philosophy is that people will always respond to the carrot and stick by trying to get more of the carrot and protecting themselves against the stick. Levinson calls this "the great jackass fallacy" because that is exactly the way one motivates a stubborn donkey. It assumes the manager with the power has the right to control and manipulate others and put them in a jackass position.[5]

A recent article in a national business magazine accurately describes this management style as it talks about the CEO of one of America's largest corporations. "_____ pays well and spills blood often: 'He motivates through a combination of fear and money.' "[6] Levinson points out this is the very approach that ignited the union movement. My experience has been that it is demoralizing and cuts off innovation. It greatly reduces productivity because one has to spend so much time choosing what to say and do to gain protection from the stick.

Lording it over others is an overpowering and domineering style of secular leadership; it is far from the Christlike way to manage and motivate people. Jesus' idea of greatness and leadership is expressed in His teachings to His disciples: "You know that the rulers of the Gentiles [referring to the Romans] lord it over them, and their high officials exercise authority over them. Not so with you. Instead, whoever wants to become great among you must be your servant."[7]

Remember, serving others begins with supporting others.

ELEVEN

Compliment, Don't Criticize

Praise people in their peaks. Raise them up in their valleys. It builds good will and productivity.

I am not talking about buttering up your people, damning them with faint praise. Neither am I talking about giving a pat on the back or the neck and shoulder squeeze as you greet your people at a social. It does not involve being your own public relations firm at the expense of getting the job done.

The caring manager verbalizes sincere praise, the kind that compliments a person for a *solid* accomplishment, whether it be the company's housekeeper for having a clean bathroom or your secretary for typing a rushed memo on time.

Practice praise. Recognize your people's accomplishments. Call them by their first names and do it in front of the big-

big boss. Use "purr-words" that express both pleasure and professionalism.

"Bill, you handled that meeting very professionally." Or "Liz, I walked into the bathroom and the chrome on those sinks was shining so bright." "Vicki, you always stay so calm and cool under pressure. I appreciate your good work."

Praises with "purr-words," not criticism with "slur-words," are what motivate people; it is what they cherish most in their memories about work. It is a well-known fact that when people retire, they usually take those written notes and momentos of praise with them. That tells us to put those exceptional, well-deserved compliments in writing.

Criticism Squelches Motivation

One technically brilliant, machine-oriented chief executive of a large company feels this way about praise: "They are supposed to do a good job; that is what they get paid for. Why praise people for doing what they are supposed to do?" He often criticizes but rarely compliments. Machines go all-out for him, but people don't.

There is a better way. It is embodied in the sixth caring command. *Compliment, don't criticize* your superiors, peers, or the people you supervise in the face of others. They are smart enough to know if you do it to others you will do it to them. They know that when you are pointing the finger at someone, you are pointing three fingers at yourself.

As wise pundit E.W. Hoch wrote:

There is so much good in the worst of us,
And so much bad in the best of us,
That it hardly becomes any of us,
To talk about the rest of us.[1]

Two types of criticism prevail in American business. Neither are productive. First is a blatant and bitter open criticism. Second, there is a more subtle, manipulative type that camouflages its deceit. Both say, we judge others to make ourselves feel and look better. The former is easy, the latter more difficult to recognize. How can you tell the difference? There is no better teacher than real life.

Two executives were trying to reach the same next rung on the ladder of success. Both were unusually competent and did their jobs well. The only difference in their management styles was the amount of noise they made climbing the ladder. One was aggressive and outgoing in flaunting his success. His implied authority on a subject often far exceeded his understanding. His clothes, his office, and his demeanor spoke loudly.

The other executive was conservative, less outgoing, and chose the appropriate review times with management to talk about his accomplishments. He had a spartan character; his clothes, manner of speech, and office reflected an austere appearance.

As the years passed, the more aggressive executive became jealous of his peer's numerous successes. He felt he was losing his footing on the climb up the ladder, and so began to take "digs" at his more successful peer. He once commented about his rival, "He has the personality of a Sherman tank, and his character and office have as much charm as a broom closet."

These sort of comments often brought a chuckle. Gradually he captivated the senior management with these clever quips and innuendoes. He eventually undermined the credibility of his peer as a leader and won the higher position. He won it through shrewd political manipulation and deception.

Is this the way to get ahead in the business world? It is for. those who reject the sixth commandment of caring. Those who choose this route need to beware of what can happen.

Daddy Warbucks, that wise businessman in the cartoon strip, "Little Orphan Annie," offered sound advice to those who choose not to care, "You don't have to worry about people you step on as you go up the ladder, unless someday, you are forced to go back down."[2]

Jesus offered more than sound advice; He delivered authoritative teaching which applies as well in twentieth-century Business America as it did in first-century Palestine: "Don't criticize people, and you will not be criticized. For you will be judged by the way you criticize others, and the measure you give will be the measure you receive. Why do you look at the speck of sawdust in your brother's eye and fail to notice the plank in your own? How can you say to your brother, 'Let me get the speck out of your eye,' when there is a plank in your own? You fraud! Take the plank out of your own eye first, and then you can see clearly enough to remove your brother's speck of dust!"³

Managing Criticism

Good managers don't tolerate negative criticism of others. They don't let it float around the office, hide in huddled groups, or lurk behind closed doors. Caring managers bring it out into the open and stop it then and there.

Ellen, a manager friend of mine, tells how criticism by a peer was handled in a company that manages with Christian principles:

> It was a strange telephone conversation I didn't understand at first. The voice said: "Ellen, this is John. I owe you an apology with regard to some criticism I made of you. I was upset over something you had done in your work, and I said some things about you in front of others. In the future, if I have a problem with anything about your work, I'll handle it with you personally."
>
> I thanked John for the call, still not fully understanding what brought it about. I found out later that someone had overheard John's critical remarks of me and discussed it with his manager—and thus the phone call.
>
> Thinking about the situation, I came to appreciate what had happened. It is very comforting to know you work in an environment where you can't be "blindsided" or undermined—where you

can trust management to support you. It makes me want to work a little harder to keep that trust.

I know a pastor who manages criticism in his church still another way. He says, "If you don't like what I am doing, be sure to tell me before you tell everyone else. Otherwise suffer, because I won't know." That's one approach for nurturing "one on one" cooperative and constructive criticism. It's an approach for maintaining the spirit of teamwork.

As a manager you must recognize that sincere praise may be the most effective motivator of all. Everyone wants it; everyone needs it. Negative criticism, on the other hand, can be debilitating. With criticism we are judging others to make ourselves look better. But with compliments we are judging others to make them look better. That is the productive way—the Christian way.

TWELVE

Humility, Practice and Promote It

It is not that Harry Truman didn't think much of himself. He didn't think of himself at all. He practiced a unique brand of humility as his daily prayer shows:

> Help me to be, to think, to act what is right, because it is right; make me truthful, honest, and honorable in all things. Make me intellectually honest for the sake of right and honor and *without thought of reward for me.* Give me the ability to be charitable, forgiving, and patient with my fellowmen—help me to understand their motives and their shortcomings—even as Thou understandest mine!'

He said the prayer as a young boy—in his high school days

as a window washer, bottle duster, and floor scrubber in a drug store. He said this prayer as he started his career—as a timekeeper on a railroad contract gang, as a newspaper employee, and as a bank clerk. As a public official in the halls of congress, he used this prayer. Finally, he said this prayer as President of the United States of America.[2]

He truly was a nobody who put his own importance and ambition aside to become a somebody. This strong sense of humility is credited with making Truman a great President. Unblinded by his own importance, he could see problems and opportunities more clearly and thus make better decisions.

This perspective is reflected in Japanese management which believes that by removing yourself from the picture you can gain greater insight. When not blinded by your ego, you can see the full possibilities. They practice it not just in decision-making but in daily interactions with their people.[3]

A Japanese company's most senior manager will often sit, not at the head of the conference table, but at the side to conduct a very important meeting. This seating arrangement does two positive things. It puts him on an equal level with his subordinates and it relaxes them. Second, it encourages everyone's participation in discussion since they are all talking with each other rather than to someone at the head of the table.

A prime example is the president of Toyota Motor Corporation, Shoichiro Toyoda. Disarmingly modest, he talks about Toyota being "an average company," though it has over 50 percent of Japan's auto sales, is close to being the number one imported car in the U.S., and ranks third in the world market. *Fortune* describes his management style: "Like many Japanese chief executives, Toyoda prefers to be seen as a president rather than a ruler. Those who know the company say he is the final decision maker in a corporate structure that depends chiefly on consensus. 'There's a saying at Toyota,' recalls a former employee: 'Slow decision, quick action.' "[4] Also, there's a sign at the gate of Toyota

City in Japan that says it all, "Every worker is a brother." It is more than a mere slogan; the president of Toyota believes it and practices it.

Humility makes a strong manager even stronger. It has a strange way of motivating others. Employees say, "She's human. She can make mistakes." "He doesn't put himself on a pedestal and look down on me. He needs my help and I am going to give it to him."

When Bill Pollard was elected President and Chief Executive Officer of ServiceMaster, one of the first things he did was visit his key managers throughout the country to get their ideas on how his office could make better contributions to the company. That's unusual. That's humility. It was a gesture that gained the help, as well as the respect, of his managers.

Recently Pollard and his Vice President of Personnel, Bill Hargreaves, agreed to change the title of the latter to the Vice President for People. Excited with his new title, the V. P. for People had that put on his license plate. Contrast that to the CEO of a large company who drove a Mercedes Benz 450SL. On his license plate were the three initials of his name followed by the Roman numeral one. Now, I ask you: From which of these CEOs would you buy a used car? With which of these CEOs would you go into battle? For which of these companies would you like to work?

What Humility Is Not
Frederick Buechner has an interesting definition of what humility is not:

> Humility is often confused with the gentlemanly self-depreciation of saying: "you're not too good at something"—when you know perfectly well you are, conscious or otherwise, this kind of humility is a form of gamesmanship.
>
> If you really aren't too good at this something, you're apt to be rather proud of yourself for ad

mitting it so humbly. This kind of humility is a form of low comedy.[5]

The extreme of humility is arrogant pride and it comes from a lofty ego—too much self-love, self-centeredness, and selfishness, at the expense of others. It leads to climbing the ladder of success in a company simply to "acquire power, status, wealth, and the control of many others"—only pretending to have "ethics, humility . . . and a concern for others." Sampson calls it the "power concept" in *How to Survive the Business Rat Race,* and it is not his recommendation for success.[6]

Humility is managing without an inflated ego or selfish authority, the two strong characteristics of the power concept. The pin-striped executive who managed as if he knew the name of "the unknown soldier," the egotistic junior executive who forced out the man that hired him, and the CEO whose Mercedes Benz plates boldly proclaimed his status are all prime examples of the power concept in practice.

Humility, practice and promote it. Following this caring commandment will allow you to manage without pretense, without show, and without thought of reward. It will win the help of others. It is a sign of strength, not weakness. It is the mark of great and enduring leadership. Practice humility, not the power concept. Do this and you will fulfill the seventh commandment of caring. There is no better example to follow than Jesus Christ, "who, being in very nature God, did not count equality with God something to be grasped, but made Himself nothing, taking the very nature of a servant, being made in human likeness. And being found in appearance as a man, He humbled Himself and became obedient to death—even death on a cross!"[7]

THIRTEEN

Recognize and Respect the Accomplishments of Your Peers

With this chapter we turn to the eighth commandment of caring. *Recognize and respect the accomplishments of your peers.* In your work compete against a standard of excellence and not against pressure from your peers. This is the ultimate test for brotherhood and teamwork. When you can sincerely compliment someone in competition with you for attention, favor, or promotion and recognize that person in front of the "big boss," then you have passed the test. To borrow a phrase from Mark Twain: "This will gratify some and astonish the rest."

This can be one of the toughest commandments of caring to practice as a manager, because it usually goes against one's ego to promote the interest of others. It is certainly one of the strongest tests of our Christian faith in the workplace. It is here that the rubber meets the road. There are no pat answers, no steps one, two, and three for carrying out this commandment of caring. But there are some guiding and inspirational examples.

Jesus Christ and John the Baptist working together provides us the best example. Here are two leaders, close to the same age where rivalry is the strongest, who brought strength and clarity to their mission. These two drastically differed in their appearances, personalities, life, and management styles. As leaders with strong followings they could have been in competition with each other. Yet they cooperated with each other. John, putting his own importance aside, recognized the leadership of Jesus and willingly shared his influence without a trace of jealousy. Jesus affirmed the teachings of John the Baptist and publicly recognized and respected the accomplishment of His peer. They both succeeded.

On the desk of the President of the United States stands a small silver plaque that says: "There is no limit to what a man can do or where he can go if he doesn't mind who gets the credit." The message echoes the same sentiment as the previous example.

A Different Kind of Competitiveness

This commandment of caring, giving credit to your peers, is not in any way meant to lessen the role of competitiveness in Business America. That is the driving force in our capitalistic society and we must preserve it—whether it be a company making a better product or an individual achieving greater success. The commandment does, however, address the way an individual goes about competing and achieving greater success.

In the workplace promote a spirited, healthy competition, but not the kind where you jockey for position, damn, or undercut others to get ahead. Remember, compete against a standard of excellence in your work—not peer pressure.

Dr. Dennis Waitley, the national authority on high level performance and personal development, defines "true winning" as "no more than one's own personal pursuit of individual excellence. You don't have to get lucky to win at life, nor do you have to knock other people down or gain at the expense of others."[1]

I knew a well-respected vice president of manufacturing who would often sit in meetings with his peers and say kiddingly, "I think that is a good idea if you let me tell the CEO it is mine." Then later in meeting with the CEO, he always gave credit to its true source. He was in a quiet, but known to be fierce, competition with the vice president of marketing for the presidency of this top *Fortune* 100 company. In staff meetings, though, he often acknowledged the marketing department's fine advertising and expressed this to the CEO.

One of his close business associates, who desperately wanted him to be president, asked him one day why he promoted his competition. The v.p. of manufacturing looked somewhat puzzled (as if to say why not?) and responded, "Well, it's true that my wife and I enjoy watching the TV commercials. Besides, if my competition gets the job, he will have my respect for being objective and recognizing good work; if I get the job I'll have his respect for being complimentary. Always remember, there are more than enough rewards (glory and money) for all of us if we recognize and support one another."

It was only a few years later that the v.p. of manufacturing became the president. And guess what—the company's advertising got even better.

A Living Example

One of the most moving examples of this commandment of caring is taken from the world of professional football where teamwork is regularly promoted and nurtured. It involved the relationship between Gale Sayers and Brian Piccolo, two running backs for the Chicago Bears in the late 1960s.

They were opposites in many ways. Gale was black, raised in Omaha, Nebraska's ghetto. Brian was white; he grew up in affluent Ft. Lauderdale, Florida. Gale was terribly serious and shy. Brian was hilariously outgoing. Gale had a natural athletic ability with size and speed. Brian lacked the same natural talents, but made up for it with courage and determination.

Both were exceptional football players. Gale made All-American at the University of Kansas and set a Big Eight career rushing record. Brian made All-American at Wake Forest and led the country in rushing and scoring in his senior year. From the beginning their rivalry was highly intense as they competed for the starting tailback position with the Chicago Bears. Gale won it and Brian became his back-up. Gale immediately began to set league rushing records with his long touchdown runs. Brian gave strong "fill-in" performances when Gale was tired and good naturedly kidded Gale with his favorite line: "I won't get you sixty [meaning sixty yards in one run], but I'll get you ten sixes"—and then burst out laughing.[2]

Despite their rivalry, they became friends and supported each other. One season Gale had a serious knee injury and after a major operation was making a slow comeback. It was in the early part of the year and the sport writers had written him off. Gale writes about the support Brian gave him: "He was one of the few guys who seemed to have confidence in me, who built up my morale. He would read what they were saying about me and he'd say, 'Don't worry about them. You're running fine. The holes aren't there, you know, just keep your chin up.' Which I was trying to do, but it wasn't always easy."[3]

Gale Sayers went on to prove he was one of the greatest running backs in the history of professional football. In 1970 he was honored by the Professional Football Writers Association, receiving the George S. Halas award as the "Most Courageous Player" in pro football. At the banquet to receive the award, Gale showed he lived the philosophy he believed, by thinking of his friend, teammate, and backup, Brian Piccolo—whose football career was suddenly interrupted by cancer. Following is an excerpt from Gale's speech at the banquet:

> I had wanted Brian to attend with me if he was strong enough, but the day I arrived in New York was the day Brian and Joy [Brian's wife] left the hospital to go back home. He had finished a series of cobalt treatments and the doctors said he could spend a few weeks at home, then return to the hospital for more treatment.
>
> One reason I wanted Brian with me at the banquet was that I intended to give him the trophy right there. But at least I was able to tell the audience something about Brian Piccolo.
>
> "He has the heart of a giant," I said, "and that rare form of courage that allows him to kid himself and his opponent, cancer. He has the mental attitude that makes me proud to have a friend who spells out the word courage twenty-four hours a day of his life."
>
> I concluded by saying, "You flatter me by giving me this award but I tell you here and now that I accept it for Brian Piccolo. Brian Piccolo is the man of courage who should receive the George S. Halas award. It is mine tonight, it is Brian Piccolo's tomorrow . . . I love Brian Piccolo and I'd like all of you to love him too. Tonight, when you hit your knees, please ask God to love him."[4]

Gale Sayers richly deserved his award, but he felt it more properly belonged to his peer, Brian Piccolo, who died shortly afterward at the age of twenty-six. The relationship between the two players is a wonderful testimony to the power of mutual recognition and respect. Sayers' philosophy of putting the Lord first, his friends (peers) second, and himself third is an excellent model for guiding our relationships in the professional world.

FOURTEEN

Interest Others
in What They Can Be

Human potential is the greatest untapped natural resource
in the world today. Consider the story of the student who
after making very good grades in high school, enrolled in a
university and made straight Ds her first semester. A counselor met with the student to discover what had happened.
Why had she suddenly turned from a good student in high
school to a poor one in college?

The student offered this explanation: "I have a low IQ."

"How do you know that?" asked the counselor.

"Well, when I took the college entrance exam, I saw the
score of 98, and I know that it takes an IQ of 118 to 120 to
get through college," replied the student.

With relief and laughter, the counselor said, "That's not
your IQ score. That's your scholastic aptitude score. That
means that out of all the students applying for college, you

were in the 98th percentile. There were only 2 percent who were brighter than you. You're brilliant!'"[1]

The next semester the student made straight A's! You are what you think you are. If you can show and encourage a person that they have the resources to be more, that opens their world to be so much more. Expectations make the difference.

If you can promote or change people's expectations of what they can be, you can change their behavior and they will achieve far beyond their potential. Expectations are those things which we hope will happen. They grow out of needs and wants. People's expectations may be explicit and conscious or implicit and unconscious. Take advantage of this facet of human personality. Practice the ninth commandment of caring. *Interest others in what they can be.* Find and promote their distinctive talents. You will be surprised at what you discover.

Surveys show that 92 percent of top and 89 percent of middle management in American corporations believe their expectations have a very important impact on their career successes.[2] Such statistics demonstrate the critical role attitudes play in developing potential.

People's talents are either natural or developed. Natural talents are those abilities with which one is born. Most often we acquire talents through the practice and development of them. Then with the Lord's help and encouragement of others, we are able to use them successfully in relation to our own needs as well as those of a company.

Everyone has distinctive talents. As a manager, you must help your people find their distinctives and encourage them in further development. This will give them a vision of their potential.

The Master's Model
Jesus was a master at spotting such key potential in His disciples, seeing their strengths and weaknesses, and shaping and molding them into greatness. With Peter, He recog-

nized early on the leadership strengths, but He saw him as being too self-assertive. Peter was too demanding of recognition, and overreaching in trying to go beyond his capabilities. He was guilty of trying to go it alone and be something that he was not. But through the instruction and support of Jesus, Peter learned not to rely solely upon himself. Peter made the discovery that every Christian has made: by yourself few things are possible, but with God, nothing is impossible. It was after this revelation that Peter gradually became the recognized leader of the church.

In Andrew, Peter's brother, Jesus saw and nurtured a sharply different potential. He appreciated the selflessness of Andrew, a man who did not seek after the leadership of the disciples nor the limelight of fame. Andrew embodied the essence of Jesus' teaching on servanthood. So Jesus helped Andrew develop into a "facilitator," one who would assist others in accomplishing their work. In today's terminology, Andrew would have been characterized a "lightweight" by many business people. However, Jesus saw a special potential in him and trained Andrew for His purposes. The Christian world today remembers Andrew as a saint who served to his fullest potential.

Jesus must have had His hands full with the powerful, selfish ambitions of James and John. But He knew that power could be good or evil, according to the heart of the person who used it. He redirected the brothers' tenacious temperaments, teaching them that real power is found in selflessness. Transformed by His technique, they became pillars of the early church.

Finally, Jesus showed Matthew the futility of a life which aimed only at heaping up riches. Instead of collecting taxes and using his pen to keep a ledger, Matthew collected the sayings of Jesus and penned a Gospel account of His life. Jesus apparently knew the distinctive talents of Matthew and how to put them to use.

The transformation of these simple lives gives ample testimony to the successful strategies of Jesus. The master manager modeled peoples' lives by inspiring His followers to greatness. No doubt, Jesus recognized that the triumph of His kingdom, in human terms, depended largely on the extent of His success in preparing and equipping the Twelve.

Find That Little Difference

William James, American psychologist and philosopher, contended that there wasn't much difference between one person and another, but what little difference there was, was awfully important.

Obviously the simplest way to find *that difference* is to observe a person's strengths and then discuss his or her expectations based upon your observation. This starts the process of the person thinking about his or her interests. More specifically, ask the person to answer three questions and address one open-ended statement. Try the ones I suggest below. Allow one written paragraph for each answer:

1. What is it that excites you the most? What causes you to feel deep joy?
2. What is it that gets you uptight? What causes you to lose sleep?
3. How do you want to be remembered?
4. I would like to plan my career, so that I may someday

_____.

Encourage the person, in completing this statement, to answer from the heart, rather than the head. You are seeking honest answers, not the common canned variety. Most importantly, let the person find and set his or her own direction and goals.

Emphasize that self-development in a career is a lifetime program. It is a day-by-day working process. The idea is to get the person feeling that he or she can be so much more. This sets the right environment for motivation of the person's self-development.

Miller and Mattson write about a more formal, structured

approach along these lines in *The Truth about You.* They offer consultation services to help people discover their gifts and direction for their lives. This is the way they describe their technique:

1. Our contention is that you have a design of your own—God's blueprint—and can only be fulfilled when you carry out that design, regardless of how high or low on the ladder of success you are.

2. We seek a description of the essential pattern that resides behind a person's talents and determines how and when they are used. We aim at knowing that fundamental part of us that needs to be fulfilled before we can believe our talents have value.

3. In order to discover a person's pattern, (we) examine only those actions which he or she feels are accomplishments that resulted in personal satisfaction.[5]

Such information forms a basis for one's motivational pattern and points the way toward work or an activity which allows one to use it. It makes a lot of sense to me. You and your company may find this approach worthwhile, particularly for those people who are struggling to find a more productive niche in their careers.

Most people work hard today for the betterment of themselves tomorrow. Such an attitude begins with having expectations of success. People may not always be realistic about success. And sometimes they are even clearly ignorant of the perils of success. But history and experience teach us that people can, like the underachieving student, attain far beyond their abilities. *Interest your employees in what they can be,* by finding and promoting their distinctive talents, and they will excel to heights previously unknown in response to your practicing this command of caring.

FIFTEEN

Self-Control, Have Patience with People

A recent issue of a business weekly quoted the CEO of a large national company in expressing his words to manage by: "Agree and commit, disagree and commit—or just get the hell out of the way."[1] This succinct statement summarizes one management philosophy. Of course, its tone runs counter to the approach I have been suggesting so far. I quote it here for a more particular purpose. The CEO's demeanor falls flat, because it is an example of management out of control.

His approach to conflict resolution is fatally one-sided. The "agree with me or get out of here" spirit does little to foster intimate relationships with employees or peers. In fact, such an attitude usually creates more conflict. When confrontation arises, the caring manager will remember still another command.

Managing Confrontation

The key to self-control and managing confrontation is putting your self-importance aside. You must forget your damaged feelings and pummeled pride and take on the challenge of forgiving and nurturing those with whom you come into conflict. Practice *self-control, have patience with people,* and so fulfill the tenth commandment of caring.

Confrontation breeds confrontation. Harsh words spoken call for harsher words in return because feelings are involved and self-esteem is at stake. This, too often, is the human pattern of conflict resolution. This flawed approach fails in the business world. Individuals never win and the organization always loses. The one whose decision "carries the day" creates a hostile "we against them" environment that is charged with tension and unproductive for settling future issues. The one whose position is not favored awaits the day to even the score. The result for the organization is one step forward and two steps back. However, as I have indicated, there is a more effective way to manage confrontive situations.

It may have to start off with an apology by you, if warranted. It could begin with you calmly asking the question, "What would you like to see happen?" A compromise on your part may be called for. Solomon offers some wisdom here: "A gentle answer turns away wrath."[2] It certainly includes a conciliatory tone of voice and manner that overcomes distrust and hostility. Humor, particularly if relevant to the issue, can often diffuse a charged situation but is never the resolution of it.

I propose that the true test of a manager involved in conflict is not how he holds his own in the confrontation, but rather the sensitivity he expresses toward others while promoting the position he believes to be in the best interest of all.

Again, Jesus offers a model we can follow. In facing the hostile and confrontive attitude of Simon the Zealot, He chose not to meet him on equal terms creating a "win/lose" situation. And likewise, Jesus never argued with Thomas in confronting his doubt. In both cases it was the patient presence of Jesus that helped these disciples to accurately understand His nature and mission.

Such an approach works in today's business climate. We can learn much from the successful art of Japanese management who fervently believe and practice the concept of "saving face" in working with each other. Our differences with them are due to environment and training, not humanity. Pascole and Athos describe it well in their book, *The Art of Japanese Management: Applications for American Executives:*

> Part of our drive for explicitness stems from the Western notion that it's a matter of honor to "get the cards on the table"! The assumption is that no matter how much it hurts, the "truth" is good for you, and it is a sign of strength and maturity to give and take negative feedback. . . .
>
> The need to "speak the truth" bluntly often masks a self-serving sense of brute integrity and macho power. Such acts of "clearing the air" are often more helpful to the clearer than to those who are starkly revealed. At a deeper level, it (brute integrity) has a sexist component. In our culture, simple straight forward confrontation—a kind of *High Noon* shoot-'em out—is mixed up with notions of what masculinity should be. Unfortunately, shoot-'em outs work best when the other guy dies and the movie ends. If you've got to work with the person again and on a continuing basis, overly "straight" communication can complicate life immensely. . . .³

It has been my experience that table-pounding and hallway shouting loses the listener's goodwill, open-mindedness, and receptivity to change. "Talking down" to a person won't draw the best productivity out of him or her. But telling it like it is with self-control and skillful expression will. Many American executives ignore this part of their development. They either falsely believe that confrontation is needed to keep morale charged up, or else they cower in the face of conflict hoping it will pass since they lack the courage to face it.

Managing Your Emotions

The personal management of emotions, for you the manager, is a crucial concern. How are you to exercise self-control? There are numerous methods being touted for business people to effectively manage their tensions. Popular responses include taking a "who cares?" attitude, practicing deep-breathing exercises, or repeating mantras in mystical meditation. Such approaches may provide instant relief, but at best they are temporary and superficial. They fail to provide the deep and durable self-control necessary for long-term productive leadership.

The key to controlling your temperament for maximum effectiveness is a peaceful mind. Nothing brings about and sustains this more than prayer. Communion with God develops an inner calming power. Prayer refocuses one's attention from worshiping self to serving the needs of others. It is a spiritual discipline. When practiced regularly it can pre-empt emotional conflicts with people. Prayer can be the manager's soft weapon, dulling confrontation and blunting conflict. In prayer we learn that self-control is equivalent to God-control.

Prayer can help you better manage those outside pressures which you have no control over. Very simply stated, you have two choices: "fight with it" or learn to relax and "flow with it." You can exert hostile energies or you can draw on that inner calming power and manage situations in a civilized fashion.

Florence Griffith-Joyner, 1988 Olympic gold medalist, has

said this about her running: "It was only when I learned to relax and let go, instead of fighting it, that I began setting world records."[4] She learned to flow with it. A sailboat runs smoothly and with dignity when in full sail, not when its sails are fighting with the wind. An eagle soars the highest when it flows with the wind and not against it. That is when you as a manager are at your best—when you flow with it and don't fight it.

I recall a CEO of one of America's largest corporations who demonstrated self-control so effectively to me. He was not terribly talkative, feeling that one could tell more with economy than excess gyration. He was a master of the "pregnant pause" in seeking to elicit workers' input on issues. He would then listen carefully, taking what one had to say seriously. He never insisted on his own ideas simply to prove he was in charge.

One afternoon the CEO called a meeting with the executive vice presidents of manufacturing and marketing to expedite the national expansion of a very successful product out of test markets. Timing was critical in this product category where those first in the marketplace with a new idea would get the biggest market share.

The problem was supplying the product to the marketplace to coincide with the availability of prime time television advertising. After more than an hour of discussion, the head of manufacturing was unyielding in his position. He stated that he could not meet the target date because the unique features of the products required special machinery parts. Further, these were only available from West Germany where the machines had been built.

Tensions began to build, and the CEO could clearly sense the defensiveness on the part of his manufacturing manager. The man's pride was at stake since he was newly appointed, and this was his debut in more than just a routine problem. To make matters worse, the CEO had come up through manufacturing and knew the area well. This made the manufacturing head feel even more apprehensive and vulnerable.

Realizing the dilemma, the CEO calmly asked, "Have we considered all the alternatives?" He didn't say, "Have you really considered all the alternatives?" That would have put even more pressure on the self-esteem of the manufacturing manager. Instantly and sounding almost facetious, the manufacturing manager replied, "Yes, unless you want to build a factory next door." And just as fast the CEO said, "That's not a bad thought; let's pursue that."

And they did. They decided to make the parts in the company's machine shop, working around the clock. The CEO knew that had been done many years before, but he also knew how important it was to save the self-esteem of a good manager and give him the opportunity to become an even better one.

A Flash of Fire Is Sometimes Necessary

Managing with self-control is not to be equated with predictability and sameness. There are those few times when a manager has to show a "flash of fire to carry a point or arouse people out of their apathy. But this must be a deliberate, and not impulsive action."[5] Such was the case when the Prince of Peace disturbed the peace and violently drove the money changers from the temple. With that done, Jesus immediately proceeded to heal the blind and lame. It seems as if Jesus knew exactly what He was doing.

Highly skilled and matured managers develop this ability to vary their self-control depending on their reading of the person or situation. The mild-mannered CEO mentioned in this chapter had that ability and I vividly remember how he used it, first with a junior executive, then later with two senior executives.

Armed with both a law degree and a M.B.A., the junior executive was a cold, articulate, and analytical technician who one too many times questioned the CEO's carefully pronounced and patiently explained decision. Faced with such insubordination, the CEO slowly rose out of his chair in the middle of one meeting and with all the eyes in the room on him, he turned to another executive and softly, but firmly, said, "He didn't hear what I said, did he?" You can bet that junior executive heard those words!

Still another time when two managers were arguing with raised voices in front of him he said, raising his voice even higher, "Can you two not get together? When you do, see me." They were in the CEO's office within the next ten minutes with a joint recommendation.

Only when his inexhaustible patience was tiring and the situation getting out of hand, did this CEO resort to using such tactics. In a short time he developed a strong, loyal management team with successful business results. His officers "turned flips" for him and his style of management. To this day many stay in touch with him, often seeking his advice and counsel, even in his retirement. His self-control and patience with people paid off. It paid dividends then and continues to do so now in the lives of those he successfully discipled.

SIXTEEN

Treat Others with Tough Love and a Tender Touch

Tough love says we are to govern those whom we have a responsibility to nurture with a strong hand. Christian love gives it a tender touch: "Love is patient, love is kind. It does not envy, it does not boast, it is not proud, it is not self-seeking. It is not easily angered, it keeps no record of wrongs. Love does not delight in evil but rejoices with the truth. It always protects, always trusts, always hopes, always perseveres."[1] The two can work together in today's world of business where people have to be held responsible and accountable for performance and profit. *Treat others with tough love and a tender touch* is the final commandment of caring.

Responsible and Accountable Management
The theme of a recent annual report of ServiceMaster was

responsible and accountable management:

> What makes management responsible? At Service-
> Master it's the commitment of our leader-manag-
> ers to achieve growth—not simply in terms of
> tangible assets, but especially in terms of provid-
> ing opportunities for people to become all they
> were created to be.
>
> At ServiceMaster we realize that a job, a career,
> life itself is never complete, but is in a continual
> state of change and growth. So responsible manag-
> ers are accountable for the development of those
> they supervise, as well as for securing measurable
> results on behalf of those they serve. A good mea-
> sure of their effectiveness is the number of capa-
> ble people developed under their supervision.
>
> Profitability is also the responsibility of manage-
> ment. It is the way we all test our performance.
> The way we challenge ourselves. The way we en-
> sure that every part of our organization is still
> growing, is still healthy. It is the way we render
> ourselves accountable for the results of our man-
> agement responsibilities.[2]

This is a company that promotes management development through its philosophy and educational and training
programs. It is a company that encourages character development through its culture and spiritual motivation. Service-
Master promotes compassion, that deep feeling of sharing
the suffering of another. It is a company that manages with
both head and heart—with both tough love and Christian
love. Finally, this company holds people accountable for
profits. ServiceMaster is a very profitable company, rich in
many ways.

The key to such a corporate philosophy working begins at
the top of a company. Its success lies in the ability of each
manager to show that people are appreciated and their indi-

vidual performances make a difference. This satisfies the two most pressing human needs in the workplace: the need to be wanted and to be needed.

It is not enough that every person understands that business must make a profit to survive. As Waterman states in *The Renewal Factor*, "Pursuit of profit is hardly a cause that inspires loyalty or makes life meaningful for most people, unless company survival is at issue, and even then it may not be enough."³

Every person must identify with what is trying to be accomplished in their area of work to achieve that profit, i.e., how he or she belongs with and contributes to it. And a person must get the feeling he or she makes a meaningful difference. They must get the feeling their manager is saying: "I want you, I need you. I will help you succeed."

The Tender Touch

There is no better time for a manager to drive home this feeling than during a performance review. But remember this is a sensitive moment of truth for that person, and it has to be done with care, warmth, and patience. It won't work if you are stern, forceful, and distant. Much training and practice is required for a manager to be effective. Here are some of the basic "caring" ingredients that need to be included in a performance review:

1. First, get the feelings and inputs of the person as to how the responsibilities of the job are viewed. Check to see that there is a clear and mutual understanding of the job definition. This helps both parties to focus on what the job is specifically about.

   Most importantly, though, it sets the stage for discovering what the person is specifically doing to support people reporting to him or her. This important part of the opening discussion emphasizes that accountability involves a measure of effectiveness in supporting and developing others.

2. Then you must secure the person's evaluation of his or her work experience. Find out how you can help them perform better. What can the company do to help them perform better? What are their strengths and weaknesses? Where do they think their job is taking them?

   This starts the self-evaluation process which is the essence of a good performance review. It creates a positive atmosphere and provides a basis for your comments.

3. Next, as a manager who has been heavily involved with this person, you should know the person's skills and be able to tell her the opportunities to be provided to help her grow. You must though, get individual input and agreement to these self-development plans and programs.

4. Finally, identify the person's expectations for the next accountability period. In other words, develop goals the person will commit to putting in place quarter by quarter. This becomes the basis for developing and amending a set of projects with objectives that mesh between the individual and the company.

The most effective evaluation is one where the manager does a lot of listening. Above all, the manager must communicate understanding. Often people don't really say what they mean, but rather say what they feel. Managers must be able to understand those feelings. We need to ask what the person is really feeling. As managers we need to understand the language of emotion behind the language of intellect. We must involve our intuitive natures. To do this, we must be "listening with the third ear."[4] Only then can we be more responsive to people's developmental needs and in turn motivate them for greater productivity.

There is another crucial aspect to this management approach to understanding. As you listen you must put aside your own importance, opinions, and biases. Managers must learn to empathize with employees and share in their emotions. It is only in this way that you will be able to relate and respond to the real concerns of people.

Tough Love

During the performance review focus your constructive comments on the specific issues, projects, or behavior; never attack the employee personally. As Mary Kay Ash says, "Sandwich every bit of criticism between two layers of praise."[5]

Caring for the developmental needs of others means not only saying the job has to be done better, but explaining that this is the way to do it. It means recognizing the strengths of a person may be better applied to a different type of job and getting that person to consider a transfer within the organization.

Never let unethical conduct go unchecked, poor performance unnoticed, or accountability unanswered. Address them directly and openly but always encourage a change of attitude in that person to do better. There will always be those who selfishly push themselves ahead at the expense of others. No matter what results they achieve in the short term, they will in the long term do harm to a company. If it is allowed to go unchecked, it either demoralizes others or becomes an acceptable way of managing among others. Animosity festers, political infighting accelerates, and productivity suffers.

There will be those who put profit before principle. They need to learn business ethics. Others will have a scorpion-like character whose nature can't be nurtured. And you will face those who, for one reason or another, cannot achieve the realistic results mutually agreed upon for the job.

Tough love means saying, as painful as it may be, "No

more of this, enough time has been invested, enough patience has been applied, enough training has been expended. You are dragging yourself and others down with your poor attitude and performance." Sometimes drastic changes have to be made. It may even require dismissal.

Every situation varies with the individual and the circumstances. Only you as a manager know if your feelings are truly objective, if the evidence for your action is based on positive knowledge and proof, and if you have faithfully applied the "commandments of caring." Only you can answer if you have provided the opportunities for the person to become all she was created to be. Only you can judge if this person has failed or if you have failed this person.

If you are passing over someone for promotion or terminating an associate's employment, the amount of care you take will make all the difference. If you keep self-esteem intact, make the adjustment easier, and help to insure future security for the person involved, it will go a long way in determining the individual's acceptance of the situation. Most people immediately get defensive and upset when informed of such unfavorable decisions. But it is also the nature of most people to respond to genuine concern and care and eventually admit that the action taken is understandable, sometimes even in their best interests.

Jesus Christ: Tough and Tender

Jesus managed His disciples with tough love. He affirmed and promoted the Law (the Ten Commandments) with them. He insisted that they maintain standards of conduct. Christ challenged and encouraged them to strive after obedience and excellence in carrying out His kingdom mission. He never let a poor performance go unanswered—whether it was Peter's untimely sleeping, James and John's selfish aspiring for power, Matthew's greedy money-worshiping, or Judas' fateful betrayal. But at the same time, His management style stressed a tender touch. For all of His demands upon the disciples, He also expressed deep concern and sensitive caring for their needs. He desired to help them be all that God created them to be.

Christ's development of His disciples is a guiding example of how you can bring together tough love with a tender touch when managing and motivating people. He successfully demonstrated how to integrate softness, feeling, and generosity with tough-minded, realistic thought. From His example you learn to combine a corporate mind and servant heart and bring out the best in people. You can follow in the master manager's footsteps and help your people to reach their fullest potential—to be all that God created them to be.

PART FOUR
Risks and Rewards

SEVENTEEN

The Greatest Success: Giving of Yourself to Others

Servant leadership is making a positive, meaningful, and lasting difference in another person's life. It is nurturing the human nature with a "caring" attitude. It is managing and motivating others to succeed to their fullest potential. *Servant leadership* is management at its best. It is built around two powerful but too often unused principles of effective management:

(1) Managers should act as *developers of people*—not as "take charge" heroes—and help others thrive and flourish.

(2) The human nature of people wants to know how much you care before they care how much you know. *You have to nurture their*

human nature by showing your concern. The "commandments of caring," faithfully and sincerely used in managing people, do this.

If self-interest and economic growth are the driving forces along your career path, then you may well end up with a nice business position and a large bank account. If you want to elbow your way to the top while neglecting the needs of others, you may achieve a seat of prominence. But remember, it is quite possible to be a huge success in your professional life but live an unfulfilling life away from the office. As one highly successful executive described it, "With all that you have and all that you have accomplished, why then the empty feeling?"[1]

Westminster Abbey in London is the ceremonial church and shrine for England's royalty. It is full of ornate chapels and tall tombs—most with beautifully sculptured figures of the occupants. They bear the prominent names of royalty and are a clear testimony that some men and women thought they could buy glory with their power, status, and wealth. Their desire to promote themselves above others lives on even after death.

In contrast, God's Acre, a Moravian cemetery in Old Salem, North Carolina, holds small grave markers of lesser known folks inscribed with only their names and dates of birth and death. All are made of granite and of the same shape and size. They are flat; no one stands higher than the other. Appropriately, this is called the democracy of the dead, because death is that moment when all are truly equal. It is in that moment when our lives are measured, not by how well we managed to serve ourselves and succeed, but by the amount of real service we rendered to others.

Risks and Rewards
Practicing *servant leadership* in your work is no guarantee that your personal agendas will be met, you will ascend to

the top job, or you will escape the trials and pressures of everyday business life. In fact, you may endure disappointment more than you secure success, because most companies recognize and reward competency, not caring. The qualities of the head (tough-minded, realistic thought), not the qualities of the heart (softness, feeling, and generosity) are the ones that most often dominate American business.[2]

Servant leadership can make you appear vulnerable to some. There will always be those who report to you that have selfish motives and ambitions. They can misinterpret your caring attitude, judge you as a "softie," and try to run roughshod over you and your ideas. And there will be those with a scorpion-like character who will leave you stunned and angry—and wondering if it is all worth it. It is. The rewards of *servant leadership* with its spiritual purpose are far greater than its risks. The benefits are far greater than your expectations, and they are everlasting. Make no mistake, it will take time and try your patience, but in the long run it will save energy and your persistence will pay off. You'll see the increase in happiness and productivity in the people under, around, and over you when you follow the "commandments of caring." While you may not receive all the outward recognition you'd like, you will receive more inner satisfaction than you'll ever need.

Above all, your *servant leadership* will inspire devotion and give greater meaning to the lives of others. The greatest success is unselfish love—the giving of yourself to others. This is the crown of life. That is what *servant leadership* is all about. But to wear the crown you have to carry His cross.

THE COMMANDMENTS

OF CARING

Judge others first with your heart, not your head.
—Show concern for and commitment to their developmental needs.

Excite with Enthusiasm.
—Make it an opportunity to involve others. It makes ordinary people extraordinary.

Socialize, don't ostracize.
—It creates a community of interests, a closer bond between people, and a desire to support one another.

Understand people that differ from you.
—Don't look for "labels." Look at their actions, attitudes, and characters.

Support your people when they need you most.
—Particularly offer help to those under pressure or in a crisis. Then they will give their most.

Compliment, don't criticize.
—Use purr-words, not slur-words.

Humility, practice and promote it.
—Don't be blinded by your own importance. This is the mark of great and enduring leadership.

Recognize and respect the accomplishments of your peers.
—Compete against a standard of excellence in your work, not against peer pressure.

Interest others in what they can be.
—Find and promote their distinctive talents. They will achieve far beyond their abilities.

Self-control, have patience with people.
—Don't argue with hostile emotions. Practice forbearance; it pays off.

Treat others with tough love and a tender touch.
—Hold people accountable.

———————————

If you have comments or questions
you may write to the author at:

JAMES F. HIND
P.O. Box 23312
Chattanooga, TN 37422

NOTES

Chapter One

1. Michael Maccoby, *The Gamesman* (New York: Simon and Schuster, 1976), p. 178.
2. David D. Barrett, ed., *World Christian Encyclopedia: A Comparative Survey of Churches and Religions in the Modern World AD 1900-2000* (New York: Oxford University Press, 1982), p. 6.
3. Lawrence M. Miller, *American Spirit: Visions of a New Corporate Culture* (New York: William Morrow and Company, Inc., 1984), p. 131.
4. Eliza G.C. Collins, ed., *Executive Success: Making It in Management* (New York: John Wiley & Sons, 1983), p. 199.

Chapter Two

1. R.C. Sproul, *Stronger Than Steel: The Wayne Alderson Story* (New York: Harper & Row, Publishers, 1980), p. 202. The information in the following paragraphs is taken from this book.
2. Montague Brown, "An American Version of Theory X," *Health Care Management Review* (Fall 1982): p. 23.
3. 1988 Annual Report of Wal-Mart, (Bentonville, Ark.), n.p.
4. Ibid.
5. Marion Wade, *The Lord Is My Counsel* (Englewood Cliffs, N.J.: Prentice-Hall, 1966), pp. 45, 121.
6. Kenneth T. Wessner, "The Four Objectives of Service-Master," *ServiceMaster Action* (Downers Grove, Ill.: ServiceMaster Industries, Inc., 1983), pp. 1-2.
7. Carol J. Loomis, "How the Service Stars Managed to Sparkle," *Fortune*, 11 June 1984, p. 159.
8. Kenneth T. Wessner and C. William Pollard, "Address to the New York Society of Security Analysts," (Downers Grove, Ill.: ServiceMaster Industries, Inc., September 13, 1985), p. 1.
9. Kenneth H. Hansen, "Reality: That Which Gives Purpose, Zest, and Motive Power to Life," (Downers Grove, Ill.: ServiceMaster Industries, Inc., 1979), p. 14.
10. Steven Flax, "The Toughest Bosses in America," *Fortune*, 6 August 1984, pp. 18-23.

11. Ibid., p. 23.

12. Yoshi Tsurumi, "How Management Is Crippling American Industry," *The Charlotte Observer*, 7 August 1983, sec. 8.

13. "Greed Gains Ground," *U.S. News and World Report*, 25 January 1988, p. 10.

14. Matthew 22:39.

15. Robert Nisbet, *History of the Idea of Progress* (New York: Basic Books, Inc., 1980), p. 336.

16. Robert S. Bachelder, "The Lost Soul of American Business," *The Christian Century*, 24-31 December 1986, p. 1171.

17. Moneyline, *The Decline of U.S. Corporate Loyalty.* (Atlanta: CNN, 7-9 July 1987), Television program.

18. Studs Terkel, *Working* (New York: Pantheon Books, 1974), p. xxiv.

19. Robert H. Waterman, Jr., *The Renewal Factor: How the Best Get and Keep the Competitive Edge* (New York: Bantam Books, 1987), p. 283.

Chapter Three

1. Philippians 2:3-4.

2. Philippians 2:5-11.

3. Loraine Boettner, *Studies in Theology* (Phillipsburg, N.J.: Presbyterian and Reformed Publishing Company, 1964), p. 182.

4. Protestant Episcopal Church in the USA, *Book of Common Prayer* (New York: The Church Hymnal Corporation and The Seabury Press, 1977), p. 326.

5. Boettner, *Studies*, p. 182.

6. The Right Reverend W. Boyd Carpenter, D.D., *The Son of Man among the Sons of Men* (New York: Thomas Whitaker, 2 and 3 Bible House, 1894), p. 237.

7. Ibid., pp. 190-91.

8. Alfred Edersheim, *The Life and Times of Jesus the Messiah*, Vol. 1 (Grand Rapids: William B. Eerdmans Publishing Co., 1959), pp. 93-94.

9. Ibid., pp. 99-101.

10. C. Milo Connick, *Jesus, the Man, the Mission, and the Message* (Englewood Cliffs, N.J.: Prentice Hall, Inc., 1974), p. 54 and Barrett, *Encyclopedia*, p. 23. My estimate is drawn from statistics quoted in these two sources.

11. Joseph B. Tyson, *The New Testament and Early Christian-*

ity (New York: MacMillan Publishing Co., 1984), pp. 109-113.

Chapter Four

1. John MacArthur, Jr., "Matthew 10:1-4." *The Master's Men*, Panorama City, California: World of Grace Communications. Sound cassette GC2271.
2. Mark 10:31.
3. William Barclay, *The Gospel of Mark* (Philadelphia: The Westminster Press, 1975), p. 250.
4. Mark 9:38.
5. Leslie B. Flynn, *The Twelve* (Wheaton, Ill.: Victor Books, 1982), pp. 91-93. See also John 14:1-7; 20:24-28.
6. John 11:16, 14:5-6, 20:25.
7. Flynn, *Twelve*, p. 81.
8. Matthew 26:24.
9. I. Abrahms, *Studies in Pharisaism and the Gospels* (New York: KTAV Publishing House, Inc., 1967), p. 23. I have replaced the negative form: "What thou hatest for thyself do not to thy fellow," with a more contemporary version for comparative purposes.
10. Harvie Conn, "Evangelical Feminism: Reflections on the State of the Union (Part II)," *TSF Bulletin* (Sept.-Oct. 1984), p. 18.
11. Maccoby, *Gamesman*, p. 48.
12. Matthew 23:11-12 and Luke 18:14 (PH).

Chapter Five

1. Eugene Kennedy, *The Pain of Being Human* (Garden City, N.Y.: Doubleday Image Books, 1985), p. 54.
2. Harry Levinson, *Psychological Man* (Cambridge, Mass.: The Levinson Institute, 1976), p. 39; cf. Frederick Herzberg, Bernard Mausner, and Barbara Snyderman, *The Motivation to Work* (New York: John Wiley and Sons, Inc., 1959), pp. 79-83; William Foote Whyte and Melville Dalton, et al., *Money and Motivation: An Analysis of Incentives in Industry* (Westport, Conn.: Greenwood Press, Publishers, 1977), pp. 1-8 and 241-49; Alan Cox, *The Cox Report on the American Corporation* (New York: Delacorte Press, 1982), p. 309.
3. Herbert A. Otto, ed., *Explorations in Human Potentialities* (Springfield, Ill.: Charles C. Thomas Publisher,

1966), pp. xiv-xv. c.f. Levinson, *Man*, p. 7.
4. Ester Quesada and Robert A. Tyrrell, *Hummingbirds: Their Life and Behavior* (New York: Crown Publishers, 1985); *Birds of the Sun God.* (Bristol, England: BBC, 1987), Television program. The preceding story is based on information drawn from these two sources.

Chapter Six
1. John 21:15-17.
2. Waterman, *Renewal*, pp. 11, 244.

Chapter Seven
1. Mary Kay Ash, *Mary Kay on People Management* (New York: Warner Books, 1984), pp. xv, xix.
2. Tom Peters, *Thriving on Chaos* (New York: Alfred A. Knopf, 1987), p. 402.

Chapter Eight
1. Norris J. Chumley (producer). *Little Mike: A Video Portrait of Michael Anderson.* (New York: PBS, 1987), Television program.
2. Lin C. Parker, "Service to Others Is His Life's Work," *Chattanooga News-Free Press*, 28 September 1986.
3. Kathleen Deveny, "Meet Mike Quinlan, Big Mac's Attack CEO," *Business Week*, 9 May 1988, p. 97.
4. Ken Sargent, "The Bedrock of Good Management," *ServiceMaster Action* (Downers Grove, Ill.: ServiceMaster Industries, Inc., 1985), p. 1.

Chapter Nine
1. Richard Tanner Pascale and Anthony G. Athos, *The Art of Japanese Management: Applications for American Executives* (New York: Simon and Schuster, 1981), p. 120.
2. Mark 4:24, as translated by Barclay, p. 103.
3. Sargent, "The Bedrock," p. 2.
4. C. William Pollard, *This I Believe.* (Chicago: Chicago Sunday Evening Club, n.d.), Television program.

Chapter Ten
1. *The American Heritage Dictionary*, Second College Edition, (Boston: Houghton Mifflin Co., 1982).

2. Jerry Willbur, "Does Mentoring Breed Success?" *Training Development Journal* (November 1987), p. 41.

3. Harry Levinson, *The Exceptional Executive* (Cambridge, Mass.: Harvard University Press, 1975), pp. 148, 153-59.

4. Interview with Don Moers, February 29, 1988.

5. Harry Levinson, *The Great Jackass Fallacy* (Boston: Division of Research, Graduate School of Harvard University, 1973), p. 10.

6. Scott Ticer and Peter Finch, "The Boss at RJR Likes to Keep 'em Guessing," *Business Week*, 23 May 1988, p. 178.

7. Matthew 20:25-26.

Chapter Eleven

1. Bergen Evans, comp., *Dictionary of Quotations* (New York: Avenel Books, 1978), p. 282.

2. Reprinted by permission: Tribune Media Services, n.d.

3. Matthew 7:1-5 (PH).

Chapter Twelve

1. William Hillman, *Mr. President* (New York: Farrar, Strauss and Young, 1952), Frontispiece.

2. Ibid.

3. Pascale and Athos, *Japanese Management*, p. 82.

4. Joel Dreyfuss, "Toyota Takes Off Its Gloves," *Fortune*, 22 December 1986, pp. 77-78.

5. Frederick Beuchner, *Wishful Thinking: A Theological ABC* (New York: Harper & Row Publishers, 1973), p. 40.

6. Robert C. Sampson, *How to Survive the Business Rat Race* (New York: McGraw-Hill Book Company, 1970), pp. 17-18.

7. Philippians 2:6-8.

Chapter Thirteen

1. Dr. Dennis Waitely, *The Psychology of Winning* (New York: Berkley Books, 1979), p. 8.

2. Gale Sayers, *I Am Third* (New York: The Viking Press, 1970), p. 67.

3. Ibid., pp. 67-68.

4. Ibid., pp. 76-77.

Chapter Fourteen

1. Nell W. Mohney, "It's All in the Attitude," *Chattanooga News-Free Press*, 17 July 1986, Sec. J4.
2. Alan Cox, *The Cox Report on the American Corporation* (New York: Delacorte Press, 1982), p. 307.
3. Arthur F. Miller and Ralph T. Matson, *The Truth about You* (Old Tappan, N.J.: Fleming H. Revell Co., 1977), pp. 15, 19, 22, 23, and 112. The consulting company's name and address are: People Management Incorporated, 10 Station Street, Simsbury, Connecticut 06070.

Chapter Fifteen

1. Jonathan B. Levine, "Sun Microsystems Turns on the After-burners," *Business Week*, 18 July 1988, p. 115.
2. Proverbs 15:1.
3. Pascale and Athos, pp. 101-02.
4. Michael Wiseman (producer). *1988 Olympic Games.* (Seoul, Korea: NBC, September, 1988), Television program.
5. Cason J. Calloway, *What Is an Executive?* (Hamilton, Ga.: n.p. 1961), p. 8.

Chapter Sixteen

1. 1 Corinthians 13:4-7.
2. 1985 Annual Report of ServiceMaster Industries, Inc. (Downers Grove, Ill.), p. 1.
3. Waterman, *Renewal*, p. 277.
4. Kennedy, *Being Human*, p. 188.
5. Mary Kay Ash, *Mary Kay on People Management* (New York: Warner Books, Inc., 1985), p. 37.

Chapter Seventeen

1. Jack Eckerd and Charles Paul Conn, *Eckerd: Finding the Right Prescription* (Old Tappan, N.J.: Fleming H. Revell Company, 1987), overleaf.
2. Michael Maccoby, *The Gamesman* (New York: Simon and Schuster, 1976), p. 178.